WE THE SHEEPLE

If This Book Does Not Make
You Mad, Nothing Will

*My book is simply written and easy to read; for high school
students, and persons wanting a "plain English" version and
understanding of what has happened to our "once great nation."*

KEN BRAUN

iUniverse, Inc.
New York   Bloomington

We the Sheeple
If This Book Does Not Make You Mad, Nothing Will

iUniverse books may be ordered through booksellers or by contacting:

iUniverse
1663 Liberty Drive
Bloomington, IN 47403
www.iuniverse.com
1-800-Authors (1-800-288-4677)

ISBN: 978-1-4502-6400-6 (pbk)
ISBN: 978-1-4502-6401-3 (ebk)

Printed in the United States of America

iUniverse rev. date: 06/14/2011

Forward

"Oh what a tangled web we weave, when first we practice to deceive!"
This line, by Sir Walter Scott could not be more prevalent than in today's
world of deception, greed, lies, and power. The reason I am writing a book,
with the title I have chosen, is to expose the deceit and lies, perpetrated
by Global Insiders, leading the people, like sheep, to their economic and
political demise."We the Sheeple" are "sheared of our wool;" the wool the
"shearer" takes is called "taxes," and the "shearer" is "the government."
After taking our "wool," we are led to "slaughter," via "a national healthcare
plan," as "We the Sheeple" are an "expendable commodity," and once
declared non-productive, and we have no value to "The Establishment"--
"the plug is pulled."

The United States has been under attack by forces of greed, evil, and
corrupted power hungry politicians from the day of its inception. In the
very beginning, when the founders wrote the Constitution, there were
traitors, and those who wanted to establish a monarchy, but there were too
many patriots, who wanted a free society, and it was with this purpose,
perpetrated by individuals seeking absolute separation of powers within a
governing body, to insure the rights and freedoms for individual citizens
that our Republic was founded; however, the "Founding Fathers" did
not envision the masterful maneuvering and manipulation of "financial
globalist" who were able to gain control of our nation's economic, and
political systems. It happened slowly, but deliberately, and in less than
100 years, the elite international group, which dictates both domestic and
foreign policies, gained control of our government. Right before the Civil

War, the culprits captured the political parties, and never relinquished control.

My book exposes how corruption, greed and "Internationalist" changed the intent of the Constitution and how our country has evolved from a Republic to a "Marxist Democratic Oligarchy Empire". I reveal how the action of "Insiders" affects us and the future of our children, and grandchildren. I want the reader to fully understand the impact the "Elitist" have on our lives and slowly diminished our freedoms. You may think my observation of our political system is irrational, too radical, or just too hard to believe, but I asked that you reserve your opinion until after you have read the last page of this book; and challenge you to do your own research and discover the truth for yourself. Prove me wrong, if you can!

More importantly, I want you to learn "what, and who" you are, politically, religiously, and economically. You may be fooling yourself regarding where you stand politically. You may be a "progressive" and not know it, but, hopefully, this book is help you discover yourself, politically and "spiritually."

"Seek ye the truth, for the Truth shall set you free," Jesus

Acknowledgements

First and foremost, I want to thank my wife for encouraging me to write this book, even though she does not necessarily agree with comments, and opinions. Secondly, I want to thank the many friends who contributed information in assisting me with the sources I used in getting facts; especially, the one who contributed written comments, which I have used throughout the pages, and, more importantly, I want to thank Jesus Christ, my Lord, who commanded us to "Seek the truth ...." Without the inspiration I receive from the teachings of Christ, I would not have the courage to write a book that will surely cause many to attempt to discredit me, and denounce me as a dastardly person, full of hate, racism, and prejudice; none of which is true. I have made an observation of the truth, as I see it, and presented what I have learned through my own research. If I have written anything that is not true, I will be the first to apologize, recount my statement, and ask forgiveness. I hope you can handle the truth, as most people cannot.

Others who encouraged me to write this book are my children (Ken, Donna, Elisha, Shannon, and Melanie), and grandchildren. I want to give special thanks to J.J., Peyton, and Cameron, three of my grandsons. They have shown unconditional love for me and always inspire me to continue living a life for God, family, and Country. Without their love, and thoughts of their future, I would not have an incentive to expose those who threaten the future of our once great nation, and the future of those I love.

Also, I want to thank "Bruce Kolinski" for his many emailed letters, which made writing this book easier. Without Bruce's input, some of the most valuable information contained herein would have been left out. Thanks Bruce for giving me permission to use your ideas and written material.

Others I want to acknowledge for their help and encouragement are: Johnny Omohundro, Larry Becraft, Don Jordan, Bob Davidosn, Dave Jones, Ron David, Glen Verner, Jim and Karen Gambel, John McDermit, Jeff Richfield, and Wally Milham (Please note: These individuals do not necessarily share my opinions).

Regardless of what some may think or say about me, my views, and my motives, I will not apologies anything I have written, unless proven to be untrue. I have a Constitutional Right to express my views as provided by the First Amendment of our Constitution, under "Freedom of Speech." Please be assured that my views are well researched and not stated carelessly or without merit.

I do want to apologies to the reader of my book for any and all typos, misspelled words, and grammatical errors. I was in a hurry to get this book published because of the timely information included. My book was not properly scrutinized or edited, by a professional. Please accept my apology and read it for the content, knowing mistakes were made, but not in its content. I did some "copying and pasting" from the internet, but, hopefully, did it without plagiarizing, as I used such information as "quotes," and tried to give credit where and when due.

Contents

Introduction

The United States is losing its sovereignty. Our nation will soon be an unconditional member of "The New World Order," led by Marxist (sometimes referred to as " Progressives"), while the "hapless Sheeple" cling to the promises and rhetoric of pseudo-conservatives and corrupted politicians, who promise a utopia. These "political and "Imperialistic Capitalist" claim to have the answers to our economic and social problems, but in reality are members of the same "Order," who created the problems they now promise to solve. They demand that the "Sheeple" vote, or trust them, as they will meet their needs, and provide security. However, these evil "Globalists" are leading the people, like sheep to their "economic slaughter," and a loss of freedom.

The truth: "The agenda for the International-financial Coterie, i.e., "PE or Power Elitist." has been well planned for the past century, especially for the past fifty plus years, and now has reached it pivot point. The initial testing grounds were conducted in Russia, and a bloody test it was, but the Russians would not just roll over and give up their freedoms and souls, no matter how much money "Wall Street Progressives" and the financial globalist poured into the fists of the Marxists, or how harsh the conditions instituted by Lenin, Stalin and other bloody, the people resisted, and Communism by force failed."

The same principles of Marx and Engels implemented by force in the old USSR were programmed for use in America to properly prepare the American populace for the surrender of their freedoms and souls, to the whims of the "Marxist Globalist," without the Marxist ever firing a shot, without force, and without a revolution. It was done by manipulation of our currency, by legislation, an infiltration of our educational system with "Progressive Intellectuals," and a well orchestrated propaganda machine, promoting social justice. Just as the Communist predicted, we will fall from within.

The steps to convert the Untied States from free enterprise to Marxism were done slowly and deliberately. It started with the population being dummied down through a politicized and substandard education system based on pop culture, forced integration, and the removal of God from the classrooms. Americans know more about their favorite TV dramas and sport's team, than important political and economic issues. which directly affects their lives. Most care more for their "right" to eat fats and take in calories, than for their Constitutional rights. Just listen to the talking heads demanding the right to eat fries from McDonalds, rather than demanding that the government adhere to the principles and laws of our Constitution. The average person can tell you more about his/her favorite football team, than he can tell you about Agenda 21. Do you know what Agenda 21 is? No? Then you should take the time, right now, to pull it up on the Internet and read the entire Treaty (a U.N. scheme agreed to by America during Clinton's term in office). After reading this treaty, you will understand more about why I have written this book, and what the future holds for the United States, unless we can do an about face.

After fully accepting the principles of Marx and Engels, "We the Sheeple" lecture peace, and, in many cases, declare wars to force our "democracy" on others. We are blinded by pride and are fools, who think we are free.

Many of "the Sheeple's" faith in God has been destroyed, and our churches, all tens of thousands of different "branches and denominations" are, for the most part, little more than Sunday circuses and televangelists exploiting, as many as they can for personal gain. A destruction of our faith is a must for political and financial enslavement. Marxism cannot exist in a Christian environment. God must be replaced by the State. The protestant "mega preachers" could care less, as long as their lavished lifestyles are secured. These religious parasites are more than happy to sell out their souls and flocks to be on the "winning" side of one "Marxist politician" or to pseudo-conservatives, who supports "globalization (the U.N.)"over that of the United States... The congregations may complain, but when explained that they would be on the "winning" side, the church members are ever so quick to reject Christ in hopes for earthly power, and a sense of security.

The beginning of the "final chapter" of our Nation's collapse has come with the election of Barack Obama. He has been truly impressive. With the help of an apathetic and naïve voting public, he is a strong Marxist, encouraging legislation and actions that enables the government's printing and spending money at a record setting pace, as he and other "political parasites" celebrate in a world of folly and corruption. No nation has ever survived with a fiat currency, and taxation and spending out of control.

We already have a pro-Marxist income tax system and a National Bank {Federal Reserve System}, but it will be worse, as both taxes and power to the Fed is increased at a rapid rate. The announcement of a planned redesign of the tax system, by the very thieves who used this system to bankroll their thefts, as they seek an expansion of the nation's debt, and new plans to swindled hundreds of billions of dollars is on the drawing board and will soon become law; these "snakes" make the Russian oligarchs look little more than ordinary street thugs, in comparison. Marx and Engels would be proud of the progressive movement in the United States, if they were alive today.

These government and bureaucratic parasites, and elected greedy politicians, including appointees, are picked from the very financial oligarch that is responsible for eroding our freedoms. They are now gorging themselves on trillions of American dollars, in one bailout after another. They are determined to usurp the rights, duties, and powers of the people to satisfy their own selfish desires. Again, congress has put up little more than a whimper to its masters, while grabbing all the power and money they can get in their "sticky hands;" and to stay in office.

The government's political parasites commanded that GM's (General Motors) president step down from leadership of his company. That is correct, dear reader, in the land of "pure free markets," the U.S. government has the power, the self-given power, to fire CEOs and dictate it will on private enterprise. This is just another nail in the coffin of freedom and a step in the direction of Communism. Government owned and/or controlled corporations are the norm in a Communist political system. It is the opposite of free-enterprise.

Prime Minister Putin, knows Communism well, and the difference between free-enterprise and government owned enterprise, He has warned the American people not to follow the path to Marxism, as it only leads to disaster. Yes, a former Communist has warned us, but we are too prideful to listen. In fact, Putin is viewed by most American as an enemy and threat to our freedoms. While Russia is not the best example to follow, it has shown the world how a Communist controlled political system destroys individual freedoms, but few listen or care, until it is too late. The principles of Marx are appealing to workers, and the masses, as the promises of Marxism falsely promises, and is believed by many, to be a system of government which will provide security, "fairness (as defined by Progressives)," and a "political Nirvana" to the people. Apparently, even though Russia suffered 70 years of this Western sponsored horror show, "We the Sheeple" have learned nothing, as we perceive those who suffered under Communism, as foolish, drunken Russians, not the intellectuals who occupy the Western civilized countries; and so, let us, the "wise" Anglo-Saxon fools, find out the folly of our own pride the hard way, by following the same principles handed down by Karl Marx and Engels.

The American public has accepted the principle of Marx with little resistance, and only a whimper, but a "free-man's" whimper. So, should it be any surprise to discover that the democratically controlled Congress of America is working on passing a new regulation that would give the Treasury department the power to set "fair" maximum salaries, evaluate performance, and control how private companies give out pay raises and bonuses? Why should anyone be surprised that Congress passes legislation that only a few of them have read and that will employ bureaucrats to determine the healthcare individuals are to receive from the medical profession? Freedoms are being usurped while we are entertained with sports and "television soaps-operas."

Barney Frank, a sex pervert flaunting his homosexuality (of course, amongst the modern, enlightened American societal norm, as well as that of the general west, homosexuality is not only not a looked down upon, but is often praised as a virtue – just watch a little TV or go to the movies) and his Marxist enlightenment, has led our nation closer to destruction. Frank, Biden, Dodd and other Marxist are dedicated to the demise of the free enterprise system and has embraced the already established principle of Communism which is entrenched in our political system (Research: "The Ten Planks of Communism," by Marx and Engels).

"The proud American will go down into his slavery without a fight,

beating his chest, and proclaiming to the world, how free he really is. The world will only snicker."

At the end of this book, I present the solution to our problems; however, many of you will disagree with my ideas, as to how to regain our freedoms, restore our Constitution, and preserve our Republic. I am prepared for the repercussions and the adverse criticisms the progressives, the Neo Cons, and the pseudo-conservatives will thrust upon me. Let them bring it on! It may not happen because my book may never sell more than a few copies and may be suppressed as soon as anyone with status reads it. But, you know, I really do not care because I have told truth, and no one has control of me.

CHAPTER ONE:
SETTING THE STAGE FOR POLITICAL TRUTH

"IT WAS the best of times, it was the worst of times, it was the age of wisdom, it was the age of foolishness, it was the epoch of belief, it was the epoch of incredulity, it was the season of Light, it was the season of Darkness, it was the spring of hope, it was the winter of despair, we had everything before us, we had nothing before us, …."

Charles Dickens – Opening lines from "A Tale of Two Cities"

Our nation was founded on the basis of "individual freedom", and God given rights, not "rights" earned or granted, by government, but inherent by virtue of Creation. Individual liberty and the freedom to choose under the Rule of Law constitute our nation's very soul. Her soul is the basis of our government's foundation, recognizing and enumerating the freedoms granted by God. When that spirit vanishes; our freedom vanishes with it. It appears that America's soul has been placed squarely upon the auction block of international economic and social slavery and is about to vanish from sight behind the immense walls of the insanely voracious "oligarchic plantation" created by "insiders" instituting the principles of Marx and Engels... The United Nations Agenda 21 was signed by the United States in 1992 and today, years later, people are still in the dark. If you were to ask at random the question, "Have you heard of Agenda 21?" the answer would be an over-whelming "No;" although, it is being implemented in every local community. It is only one of many agreements and a treaty the US has entered into in recent years that is detrimental to our freedoms.

1

You need to read and understand Agenda 21, and the plans the Power Elitist have for your children and grandchildren. I also suggest you to read the "The Ten Planks of Communism," by Marx and Engels, which I have included in Chapter Two.

"We hold these truths to be self-evident, that all men are created equal, that they are endowed by their Creator with certain unalienable Rights that among these are Life, Liberty and the pursuit of Happiness. That to secure these rights, Governments are instituted among Men, deriving their just powers from the consent of the governed, That whenever any Form of Government becomes destructive of these ends, it is the Right of the People to alter or to abolish it, and to institute new Government."

If you believe that future generations will be governed by the philosophy of our Founding Fathers, as stated above, you are foolish and naïve. Their future, as is the present, will be dictated the "Power Elite," with a progressive philosophy, following a plan proposed in Agenda 21. The goal of Agenda 21 and the Elitist is to control the world's resources, and "reduce" global population. War is one very efficient method for 'population control! Wars are already being fought. We have the non-declared wars (unconstitutional) ones, which our men and women are fighting in Iraq, and Afghanistan, and the countless civil wars and border clashes in Africa... Nations have been taken over by "internationalist's imperialistic empire builders" whose goal is world population reduction, control of global economics, and control of all natural resources. This is their aim. While the UN speaks vaguely it in terms of population control, the "Power Elitist" states the actual objectives are far more pernicious. It is well documented, and in the open, in various places, and it appears to be coming to a head. All you need to do to learn more about the planned control of the population is a little research; I suggest that you spend more time learning about your future and less time on the couch watching "Monday Night Football." The "world ruling class," it appears, think only they have a right to rule, indeed to live a secure and wealthy life-style, at your expense....no one else will have rights except in terms of Orwellian transvalue language, if, "IT" is allowed to stand. It is not just population, but also the confiscations of lands by the Elite; and the gross energy-consuming hyperrealist civilization that these have built for themselves, buttressed by the military-industrial complex making war all over the globe, expanding their empire, at the expense of a diminishing middleclass and the poor.

Obama's Executive Branch of government, symbolized by "the people's" White House as home to our elected President does not believe, nor accept the basic spiritual concept of "equal rights under the law," or, the underlying foundational principle of "equal justice." EQUAL JUSTICE establishes our RULE OF LAW. Our Executive Branch has steadily replaced this most basic premise of human dignity with the tawdry fallacy of **"social justice,"** deceitfully offered to a voting population, they hope has been thoroughly de-educated, re-educated and devolved into an indoctrinated, dumbed down, collectivized mass of "complacent serfs. "This bloodless coup" began in earnest with the sale to voters by the world's financial oligarchy of ignorant pawn, Woodrow Wilson, and "the likes." It finally comes to fruition recently, under the carefully "nurtured pawn-ship" of Barack Hussein Obama. Herbert Marcuse wrote in the first chapter of One-Dimensional Man: "Under the rule of a repressive whole, liberty can be made into a powerful instrument of domination. The range of choice open to the individual is not the decisive factor in determining the degree of human freedom, but what can be chosen and what is chosen by the individual. The criterion for free choice can never be an absolute one, but neither is it entirely relative. Free election of masters does not abolish the masters or the slaves. Free choice among a wide variety of goods and services does not signify freedom if these goods and services sustain social controls over a life of toil and fear – that is, if they sustain alienation. And the spontaneous reproduction of superimposed needs by the individual does not establish autonomy; it only testifies to the efficacy of the controls."

Note the poignant statement made by Marcuse above: "free election of masters does not abolish the masters or the slaves". I submit to you; **we are freely becoming "socialistic slaves" by our own choice.**

Now please read the above paragraph again – only more slowly and more carefully. The concept contained in the above paragraph has led to a Progressive political strategy, which is devouring our freedom and most do not realize it. We do not freely choose our elected representatives. We freely select from a narrow, prepared menu created for us by the RNC and DNC, as developed with select ingredients provided and weighted by the "world's financial oligarchy." We freely elect only from a limited list of candidates sold to us by an indoctrinated, dysfunctional controlled media. This is the reason nothing ever gets any better for "We the Sheeple." The "supposed" representatives we vote for on both sides of the aisle have been carefully selected and nurtured to be two sides of the same coin. They are nurtured by wealth, financial power and corrupt influence; not by integrity or honor, and are best defined by the old adage, "head they win and tails we lose." Almost to a man, or woman, they certainly and obviously do not represent "we the people". Those few who do honestly represent "we the people" are virtually powerless and are relentlessly demonized by the progressive media; or in some cases, assassinated, or drummed out of office on trumped up charges.

In 1934 Herbert Marcuse, sometimes reverently referred to, as "Father of the New Left" laid out a scheme for "academic stooges" to follow, and teach that will cost us our freedoms. Marcuse a devout Marxist immigrated to the U.S. and later, after working within OWI and OSS, precursor to today's CIA, burrowed deeply into Columbia, Harvard and Brandeis Universities. He ended his destructive propaganda career, as a pipe smoking academic legend of sorts at University of California, San Diego. It's common knowledge today that American education has flat lined; conned into wasting countless billions in new Progressive de-educational spending our children which continues to fall behind their peers throughout the world in basic reading, writing, math and science – not to mention history. Why? Simply put – to render us more ignorantly complacent and immanently more desirous of becoming "feudal serfs." The plan to create a society of nitwitted progressives really gained ground in the sixties with the anti-culture movement...We are making zombies of the generations of the future, making it easier and more desirable for our youth to accept a political system that is completely "Marxist." Every person should research Arnold Toynbee; Aldous Huxley; T.S. Eliot,; W.H. Auden,; Sir Oswald Mosley; and D.H. Lawrence, Huxley's homosexual lover; and read two book, "Dope, Inc." and "The Report from Iron Mountain." If you will do this, you will better understand the challenge we and our grandchildren will face in the future, as we will soon yearn to preserve our freedoms and Constitutional Rights.

Marcuse played an instrumental role in destroying American education (as did John Dewey. Dewey was a progressive that "made truth subjective") and in the development of carefully show cased, frontal issues divisive generally to western society and specifically to capitalism and individual freedom. Marcuse and friends worked diligently, obsessively and effectively to prepare American culture for its incremental downfall. Meanwhile, John Maynard Keynes, developed economic theories which are also destructive to freedom. I gather most outside liberal academia have never heard of Herbert Marcuse, but most informed people have heard of Keynes. Not hearing of Marcuse is a powerful testament to his success. Marcuse was the devious mind behind many scenes, if not most, of today's popular "political correct issues;" those issues over which we are most likely to distract ourselves, virulently disagree or even better – over which we can actually hate each other. Then there is Keynes. Keynesian economics are well accepted and taught as "gospel" in most institutions of higher learning. When we add Keynes to the mix, with Huxley, Thomas Mann (a member of "the Club of Rome," which is a globalist organization), along with Ervin Laszlo, who wrote, " Strategy for the Future (1974)," and others from the same cult and like thinking, we discover a foundation, which was establish to destroy our Constitution and America's freedoms. The destruction was well planned and deliberate; and takes patience.

The demented Marcuse was a genius at devising social issues, which could easily be perverted into tools for the advisories of societal chaos, collectivized pseudo-cures, the destruction of economic freedom and of course the death of individual liberty. His rhetorical skill played a pivotal role in the birth and cancerous growth of such favorites as: promotion of drug use, feminism, gay rights, the haves and have not's or as we know it "class warfare", social justice as opposed to equal justice, racism and of course the "green" movement (all of which were promoted by Huxley and his cronies, who gave birth to LSD via the CIA). All of these movements, under the guise of achieving social justice for one class are intended to destroy all classes through divisive chaos leading to the eventual "State" solution and promised utopia. Of all these movements, the most powerful, most deceitful and most threatening to individual liberty is environmentalism, and "mother earth."

Rachel Carson's Silent Spring (1962) endowed her, as "Mother" of the environmental movement. I maintain that Herbert Marcuse, who argued that "authentic ecology flows into a militant struggle for a socialist politics which must attack the system at its roots, both in the process of production and in the mutilated consciousness of individuals" must then be the "Father" of this insidious hoax, which is firmly embraced by Al Gore and other progressives. The environmental movement, and social justice, wonderful on its faces, has been cruelly hi-jacked by Marxist as the single most powerful weapon in the arsenal of "collectivist control". Communism itself, of course, is the single most powerful weapon of the international financial oligarchy in establishing easily controlled "central governments" throughout the world for the convenient purpose of establishing total control via "One World Governance;"i.e., The New World Order.

Our First Lady's, the one in the White House with the "big fat butt," has a nice little garden; and her feigned caring about "fat kids" along with the dog they never had and her husband's deep, pandering caring about virtually everything under the sun is just a cheap, but effective sales job leading "We the Sheeple" to believe we have once again freely and correctly chosen valid representatives who cares and serves diligently in our best interest. Political correctness wraps the selected candidate within a protective cloak of ignorance and cowardice. The reality is that, just as George W. Bush used patriotic language, but acted otherwise on behalf of his true masters, Obama pretends to care deeply about the victims he organized, but actually just uses them for their uninformed votes to achieve the ends of his true masters. Both are puppets on the strings of international puppeteers, who have one agenda, and that is control of the world's natural resources, including population control, and establishing a "One World Government." Bush and Obama, as all Presidents since Woodrow Wilson, and some before him, have the same "masters." These "political cronies" are "phony leadership prostitutes," none really any worse than the others. They cannot be trusted to act in our best interest.

Our White House and Congress have treasonously labored for decades, with embarrassingly few courageous dissenters to sell America's soul in exchange for the largess of their international masters. **The question is "Will we, the governed continue to blindly grant our consent to the sale?"**

Had we followed Jefferson's advice and revolted every twenty years, "eliminating most of the politicians, and "elitist (one way or another)," maybe, our Republic would have stayed intact."

As it is now, our Presidents are, as Roosevelt stated, "selected, not elected." According to "The Sept. 12 guest editorial," by William Rusher ("The GOP is set") five Republican candidates were listed that he felt could easily win the nomination for president. What is interesting is that five of the Republican candidates in the last election were members of the Council on Foreign Relations, and/or the Bilderberg Group; and Mr. Rusher picked four of the five. The CFR Republicans are Mitt Romney, Rudy Giuliani,

John McCain, Newt Gingrich and Fred Thompson. Mr. Rusher, as well as the rest of the controlled media, has placed the CFR members on center stage. The Democrats are not left out at all. The CFR Democrats were Barack Obama, Hillary Clinton, John Edwards, Chris Dodd and Bill Richardson. Clinton and Obama are two that are now chosen for the next presidential race; others will be added, if needed; and this selection may change depending on the agenda of the "Elitist."

Should we worry whether candidates and appointees are CFR members or not? Yes! The CFR and its elitist members are on a fast-track course to abolish the sovereign U.S.A. by end of 2012, or shortly thereafter, literally forcing us to become part of a North American Union (by treaty or by formal recognition; however this has be so well publicized that a formation of a formal entity may not be feasible). According to some reliable sources, Mexican truckers have already been given authorization to run their long-haul rigs throughout the United States; San Antonio, Texas, is advancing the city's goal to establish itself as a North American Free Trade Agreement inland port; and a Mexican customs inspection facility is planned for Kansas City, Mo. NASCO (Tri-National Advocacy for Efficient, Secure, Environmentally Conscious Trade & Transportation) has figured out a way to cash in on the Chinese containers passing along the NAFTA superhighway from the Mexican ports of Manzanillo and Lazaro Cardenas to U.S. and Canadian destinations. The first "North American Union" driver's license, complete with a hologram of the continent on the reverse, and has been created in North Carolina. Note that all this is without congressional approval or oversight. This is just another step in unification of North America. Remember, pseudo-conservative Newt Gingrich (CFR Member) supported NAFTA (More about Newt later).

The powerful U.S. Council on Foreign Relations, along with Mexican and Canadian counterparts, launched the Security and Prosperity Partnership on March 23, 2005, at a meeting in Waco, Texas, with George Bush, Mexico's President Vicente Fox and Canadian Prime Minister Paul Martin. The tri-national agreement, hatched below the radar in Washington, contains the recommendations of the Independent Task Force of North America to remove the U.S. borders and establish a North American Union similar to the European Union and replace the dollar with a currency called the amero; or maybe some other named currency, since the amero has been publicized so much and has received adverse acceptance. With the borders unprotected, or loosely protected, we may as well have open borders now.

Then we have the number one phony conservative, John McCain saying that he wants to protect the borders, this is the same John McCain that was promoting amnesty not too long ago and stopped campaigning to fly back to Washington to vote for TARP... He, too, is a member of the CFR.

The NAFTA "superhighway" linking Mexico, the U.S. and Canada is already underway. A Texas legislator tried to stop this massive mile-wide structure, but Texas Gov. Rick Perry vetoed the bill. The governor is a member of the Bilderberger Group, with the same CFR viewpoint. The Bush administration has limited the 854 miles of border fencing called for in the Secure Fence Act to just 18 miles as part of the SPP "open border" policy. Perry is a pseudo-conservative, and is dangerous threat to our freedoms. We know liberals, but with the controlled media behind him, Perry, are painted as a staunch conservative. He has "hoodwinked" the people!

Many in Congress is just now starting to wake up by having several bills to stop the forward progress of the NAU. Nineteen states are in the process of passing legislation to stop it, as well. Twenty-two members of the U.S. House of Representatives — 21 Republicans and one Democrat — urged President Bush to back off when he attended the third SPP summit meeting in Montebello, Quebec. The Senate just voted 74-24 to pass an amendment removing funding from the Department of Transportation bill for the Mexican trucking in the U.S. What is Rep. Mike Thompson, D-St. Helena, doing? Nothing!

The CFR member actions are considered treason under the U.S. Constitution, and if you support a member candidate, then you are a problem as well. Most past presidents came from a pool of CFR members as have the most recent presidential candidates in the 2008 election. Candidates do not advertise their CFR membership to the public. They pose as "liberals" and "conservatives" to control all aspects of the debate. The CFR has really stacked the deck during the 2008 election. To bolster CFR support, the controlled media blacks out non-CFR candidates. For example, Republican candidate Ron Paul won the Maryland Straw Poll, Alabama Presidential Straw Poll, was victorious in New Hampshire and won a number of Internet polls including MSNBC, all this without a word from the press. It's because grassroots America has figured out how to get around this blackout by going to independent news organizations on the Internet and discovering that there are a real candidates supporting our sovereign nation; some of which created the "Tea Party." Unfortunately, much of the "Tea Party Movement" has been hijacked by Republican Neo Cons, who are included with creators of our economic, moral, and political decay. Whether you're on the Internet or not, don't buy into the media's portrayal of pseudo-conservatives, such as, Fred Thompson, who is portrayed as a new Ronald Reagan (Reagan was another pseudo-conservative, but most think he is the "father of the new conservative movement;" nothing could be farther from the truth). Senator, Fred Thompson voted for such things as expanding the welfare state, federal involvement in education, expanding trade with Communist nations and subsidizing abortions. By being a CFR member he supports preemptive war and would place the North American Union as a top priority, and will continue to push this agenda...Besides that Reagan was a liberal and played into the hands of the "Power Elite;" so, maybe, Fred is another Reagan!

(A "side-bar" comment) Here is Reagan's record:

As Governor, on a "conservative" platform, Reagan California's spending increased by 112%. Reagan was the first Governor to increase personal income taxes by 60%, increase the cigarette tax by 200%, and increase state tax collections by 152%; and the only president to have been divorced.

Reagan increase spending by 80%, in his 8 years, as president, and spent more in eight years than was spent in prior 50 years.

Increased the national debt faster than growth of national income.

Reagan increased the national debt, about 300%

He was the first to increase the national debt faster than growth of GDP

Reagan doubled the deficit.

He kept America a debtor nation.

During his presidency the Dow set a record for the largest one day percentage decline in the DOW in history. 10-19-87.
During his presidency the nation "real" interest rates rose to 8% after averaging 1% over 35 years.
He kept prime interest rates at 20%, for a long period of time. (This was blamed on Jimmy Carter, just as Obama is blaming Bush today – it is part the game these parasites play).

Home loan interest rates as high as 16%.

First to allow the <u>savings and loan industry to be raided</u> after signing a deregulatory bill and proclaiming "I think we have hit the jackpot". Come and get it the vaults are unguarded...

First to testify "under oath" 130 times that "<u>I don't remember</u>".

First to have <u>unemployment at 10.8%</u> since great depression.

His party led to the most <u>farm foreclosures,</u> since the depression; in <u>bank failures</u>; in <u>Savings and Loan failures</u>; the highest percent increase in <u>personal bankruptcies</u>.

Reagan was the first President to have over $10,000,000 <u>increase in personal wealth</u> from serving for 8 years as president.

Ronald Reagan cut taxes once, while raising them six times. The national debt increased, and credit expanded. Reagan was given credit for helping the economy, when the opposite was true. Federal Reserve Chairman Paul Volcker tried when he raised interest rates. That's the opposite of what Fed Chairman Alan Greenspan has done to keep inflation low. Greenspan's low interest rate policies were continued by Ben Shalom Bernanke, current Fed Chairman.

Reagan had his war also, as all Presidents want and seem to embrace, when the U.S. invaded the small island of Granada.

The greatest Reagan myth is that "He won the cold war." The truth is Reagan did nothing to bring down the Soviet Union. By 1980, the Soviet Union was trying to cut its own defense spending. Reagan made it harder for them to do so. Reagan never even tried to bring down the Soviet Union. In fact, no president has done anything to diminish the spread of Marxism. In this book, I point out how we have embraced the "Ten Planks of Communism," by Marx and Engels, in our political system. Reagan's wasteful overspending on defense didn't end the Soviet Union. In fact, it played into the hands of authoritarian "Communist" hard-liners in the Kremlin. Reagan thought the Soviet Union was more powerful than we were, so, he was trying to close what he called "the window of vulnerability." This was sheer idiocy. No general in our military would trade our armed forces for theirs. We had better systems, better troops, better weapons, and better morale, and we still had a sense of patriotic freedom.

The truth is that we lost the Cold War. The principles written by Marx and Engels formed the foundation for a global plan for the "insiders" (as they are referred to by Carroll Quigley in his book, "Tragedy and Hope")" to establish a New World Order.

The Soviet Union military couldn't deal with a weak state on its own border, the poor, undermanned Afghanistan. Afghanistan is not on our borders, and we were able to defeat the enemy there for a while; however, it has turned political and as usual, the "insiders" have decided to democratize a Muslin country, which is impossible to do. Richard Nixon told Reagan he could balance the budget with big defense cuts. Reagan ignored this, and wrecked our budget, but remember, a balanced budget is just a manipulation of numbers, What is needed is a cut in spending and a reduction of government, which is opposite of what the "insiders" want in the U.S. Mikhail Gorbachev, a pawn of the elitist, followed instruction and broke up the USSR into manageable states. Maggie Thatcher, fell out of grace with the globalist, and was replaced by Tony Blair; but, alas, worry not, they remain members of the Power Elitist.

Reagan seldom took the blame for any adversities. He even blamed Jimmy Carter for the deaths of 243 Marines stationed in Beirut, helpless and unguarded; yes, this happened on Reagan's watch. Again, let me remind you that this is part of role that Presidents in office play. Reagan was an actor playing the part of the president; it was style over substance. **Reagan was by far the most overrated man in American history, and even today, most conservatives believe Reagan was a true patriotic conservative.** NOT TURE!

"By the end of his term, 138 members of Reagan administration had been convicted, had been indicted, or had been the subject of official investigations for official misconduct and/or criminal violations. In terms of number of officials involved, the record of his administration was the worst ever." from p. 184, Sleep-Walking Through History: America in the Reagan Years, by Haynes Johnson, (1991, Doubleday). Now, let's continue our journey and look into the investigation of Reagan's association with Oliver North, another darling of the phony right (Neo Cons).

Oliver North was the director for Political-Military Affairs in the Reagan's administration. In 1986 it was revealed that a secret U.S. operation had been selling military equipment to Iran. You know Iran is a "member" of the "Evil Axis Empire," as described by George Bush.

Well, in the 80's we were selling them arms, while also supporting Saddam Hessian's Iraq. Typical of what the "insiders" will do. It is said by most "TV and Radio, Talking Heads" that North is a favorite among conspiracy buffs, who maintain that his operation took guns to Central America and brought back cocaine during the 1980s. Notice how anyone who mentions a conspiracy is labeled? Well, let's have a look at the facts, and you decide who the "buffs -nuts" are. Research North and Barry Seals, George Bush and Dan Lassiter (Clinton's drug dealing friend – pardoned by Clinton). Please do your own Internet search and discover how drugs were transported into Mena, Arkansas, and by whom (who were those involved). You will find the truth regarding who the real criminals are and how corrupt our system really is!

Here is an example of what you may expect to discover: According to Investor's Business Daily, "Sally Perdue, a former Miss Arkansas and Little Rock talk show host who said she had an affair with then-Gov. Clinton in 1983, told the London Sunday Telegraph that Clinton once came over to her house with a bag full of cocaine. "He had all the equipment laid out, like a real pro."

Then there is this: "I personally witnessed complicity between these two men; Bush and Clinton, in terms of transporting cocaine into the US for the purpose of sale to generate money to fight a war." -Terry Reed Air Force Intelligence (in an interview with Alex Jones).

Next: "What I am about to share with you should cause you great concern because this is an example of the sort of thing that goes on in Washington.

On October 5, 1986 in Nicaragua, a CK123 Cargo plane, with weapons and CIA employees on board crashed. This was the beginning of what links what I am about to tell you together. This was the start of the Iran-Contra affair. It was proven that the weapons were supplied by the CIA and destined for the Nicaraguan Contras in of the Congressional Poland Amendments. Special prosecutor Lawrence Walsh spent six years determining who in the Reagan administration was involved in the operation. Among those that were involved in this operation were **George Bush, Oliver North, Dewey Clarridge, John Pointdexter and Caspar Weinberger**." *From, "The Mena Arkansas Reagan, Bush, Clinton, Drug Connection" -September 20th 1998 by columnist David Lawrence Dewey*

The Progressive Review, AN ONLINE JOURNAL OF ALTERNATIVE NEWS & INFORMATION provides the following information regarding Clinton, Bush, Seals, and others in drug dealing and illegal money laundering but you need to read the entire article, by <u>Sam Smith</u>

"It was in the 1990s, Jenifer Flowers tells Sean Hannity's WABC talk radio show: "He (Clinton) smoked marijuana in my presence and offered me the opportunity to snort cocaine if I wanted to. I wasn't into that. Bill clearly let me know that he did cocaine. And I known people that knew he did cocaine. He did tell me that when he would use a substantial amount of cocaine that his head would itch so badly that he would become self conscious at parties where he was doing this. Because all he wanted to do while people were talking to him is stand around and scratches his head. ...."

Two Arkansas state troopers will swear under oath that they have seen Clinton "under the influence" of drugs when he was governor. Sharlene Wilson is a bartender who ended up serving time on drug crimes and cooperating with drug investigators. She told a federal grand jury she saw Clinton and his younger brother "snort" cocaine together in 1979. Jack McCoy, a Democratic state representative and Clinton supporter, told the Sunday Telegraph that he could "remember going into the governor's conference room once and it reeked of marijuana." Historian Roger Morris, in his book "Partners in Power," quotes several law enforcement officials who say they had seen and knew of Clinton's drug use. One-time apartment manager Jane Parks claims that in 1984 she could listen through the wall as Bill and Roger Clinton, in a room adjoining hers, discussed the quality of the drugs they were taking."

Then Smith further states, Major drug trafficker Barry Seal, under pressure from the Louisiana cops, relocate his operations to Mena, Arkansas. Seal is importing as much as 1,000 pounds of cocaine a month from Colombia according to Arkansas law enforcement officials. He will claim to have made more than $50 million out of his operations. As an informant, Seal testified that in 1980-81, before moving his operation to Arkansas, he made approximately 60 trips to Central America and brought back 18,000 kilograms. In 1996 the Progressive Review will report: "The London Telegraph has obtained some of the first depositions in ex-CIA contract flyer Terry Reed's suit against Clinton's ex-security chief - and now a high- paid FEMA director - Buddy Young. According to the Telegraph's

Ambrose Evans-Pritchard, "Larry Patterson, an Arkansas state trooper, testified under oath that there were 'large quantities of drugs being flown into the Mena airport, large quantities of money, and large quantities of guns.' The subject was discussed repeatedly in Clinton's presence by state troopers working on his security detail, he alleged. Patterson said the governor 'had very little comment to make; he was just listening to what was being said.'"

Roger Morris & Sally Denton, Penthouse Magazine - Seal's legacy includes more than 2,000 newly discovered documents that now verify and quantify much of what previously had been only suspicion, conjecture, and legend. The documents confirm that from 1981 to his brutal death in 1986, Barry Seal carried on one of the most lucrative, extensive, and brazen operations in the history of the international drug trade, and that he did it with the evident complicity, if not collusion, of elements of the United States government, apparently with the acquiescence of Ronald Reagan's administration, impunity from any subsequent exposure by George Bush's administration, and under the usually acute political nose of then Arkansas governor Bill Clinton"

In my opinion, I have no doubts about the CIA's involvement in drugs, money laundering, arms dealings, and corruption which involved Bush, Clinton, Seal, Dan Lassiter, and other well know characters. --- ***End of "side bar"***

Back to the subject at hand:

In contrast, Rep. Ron Paul sets himself apart from other Republicans by being decidedly anti-war while supporting American independence and sovereignty. He is referred to as "Dr. No" by his colleagues because of his refusal to support unconstitutional bills; however, he, too, "puts pork into legislation."

Yes, we must not elect official who are members for the CFR: The following is a brief background on the CFR, as presented by Carroll Quigley in his book, "Tragedy and Hope," which is one of my favorite books. Also note a little about Quigley himself, and then I will get back to Ron Paul:

Author of Tragedy and Hope (tragedy is all the people who must suffer and die for the NWO, and the hope is the NEW WORLD ORDER) Professor Quigley was a Globalist, he supported the idea NEW WORLD

ORDER and wrote about it, he, unlike the elites, thought the people should know about it.

"The powers of financial capitalism had another far reaching aim, nothing less than to create a world system of financial control in private hands able to dominate the political system of each country and the economy of the world as a whole. This system was to be controlled in a feudalist fashion by the central banks of the world acting in concert, by secret agreements, arrived at in frequent private meetings and conferences. The apex of the system was the Bank for International Settlements in Basle, Switzerland; a private bank owned and controlled by the worlds' central banks which were they private corporations. The growth of financial capitalism made possible a centralization of world economic control and use of this power for the direct benefit of financiers and the indirect injury of all other economic groups." Tragedy and Hope: A History of The World in Our Time (Macmillan Company, 1966,) Professor Carroll Quigley of Georgetown University.

"The Council on Foreign Relations is the American branch of a society which originated in England ... [and] ... believes national boundaries should be obliterated and one-world rule established." Dr. Carroll Quigley.

When Glenn Beck speaks of the CFR, and refers to it as "evil," he does it in a way that is demeaning to those who knows the truth, as it is truly and evil organization. Beck portrays members of the CFR, especially one woman, who wrote a book about Calvin Coolidge as a patriotic conservative only proves that Beck is also a phony and a liar. He will not tell the truth regarding the history of the CFR. He can't, as his boss is a member.

Regarding the "One World Organizers," Quigley wrote: "I know of this network because I have studied it for twenty years and was permitted for two years in the early 1960s to examine its papers and secret records. I have no aversion to it or to most of its aims and have, for much of my life, been close to it and too many of its instruments. I have objected, both in the past and recently, to a few of its policies ... but in general my chief difference of opinion is that it wishes to remain unknown, and I believe its role in history is significant enough to be known." (Dr. Carroll Quigley, Tragedy and Hope)

"As a teenager, I heard John Kennedy's summons to citizenship. And then, as a student, I heard that call clarified by a professor I had named Carroll

Quigley."President Clinton, in his acceptance speech for the Democratic Party's nomination for president, 16 July 1992.

Now back to Ron Paul. Some claim that Ron Paul is also an unofficial member of the John Birch Society, which was founded by Masons, funded by Nelson Rockefeller and run by Jesuit-trained Knights of Malta. In other words, the JBS is a gatekeeper organization, designed to control the opposition and make sure nothing substantial is ever done to impede the New World Order system which just keeps on rolling over humanity. If this is true, then I have been fooled for years believing a lie. Someone help me find the truth, please!

While the pseudo-conservative and so called fair and balanced "talking heads" ("the spin stops here") on TV blame the shadowy Cloward-Piven strategy as the taproot of abusive practices that triggered the nation's financial crisis, and claims that the strategy is to bring about the fall of the Free Enterprise System by overloading and undermining government bureaucracy, it is really the "International Elitists" who are responsible. If it were not for the "establishment's insiders," with their foundations donating billions of dollars to educational institutions, Cloward and Piven would have been considered nothing more than screw-ball professors following Marxist principles.

The tactics including the flooding government with impossible demands until it slowly breaks our free market system to pieces like a shattered mirror is part of a planned agenda by those who have global goals to control the world's natural resources, and make "political serfs" of most of what is left of the world's population, after population control is escalated... You must read about the desired number of people the Globalist plan to have as a world's total population... A wave of corrupt, naïve, and Marxist politicians, many of them bogus conservatives; have sacked banks, forced the Department of Housing and Urban Development for affirmative-action to allow borrowing by unqualified individuals; and, then, pulling down the national financial system by demanding exotic, subprime mortgages for low-income Americans with little hope of repaying their loans. The destruction of America is at hand...

A little more about Cloward and Paven: One of the plans used by the Elitist was developed in the mid-1960s by two Columbia University sociologists, Andrew Cloward and Frances Fox Piven may well have been inspired by Karl Marx and Fredrick Engels. Some of their strategy was drawn from Saul Alinsky, Chicago's notorious revolutionary Marxist community organizer. The Association of Community Organizations for Reform Now (ACORN) succeeded the National Welfare Rights Organization in the execution of the Cloward-Piven grand tactics of using minorities, the poor, and the naïve, to tear down the capitalist system. It was low-income, mostly black and Hispanic people, who were used by ACORN Marxist to take subprime toxic mortgages. However, do not listen to Glenn Beck's half-truths because without the help of the Power Elitist, failure could not have been made possible.

"The Congress....Desirous...to have people of all ranks and degrees duly impressed with a solemn sense of God's superintending providence, and of their duty, devoutly to rely...on His aid and direction...Do earnestly recommend Friday, the 17th day of May be observed by the colonies as a day of humiliation, fasting, and prayer; that we may, with united hearts, confess and bewailed our manifold sins and transgressions, and, by sincere repentance and amendment of life, appease God's righteous displeasure, and, through the merits and mediation of Jesus Christ, obtain this pardon and forgiveness."
> — The Continental Congress, May 16, 1776

My, how much change we witness in attitudes of elected officials; from our founding elected officials respecting God, to the current politicians, who degrades His name in profane language. I cannot find any quotes made by our Founding Fathers using profanity to emphases a point or position, as Joe Biden did during the Presidents acceptance speech. I do not see evidence that our Founders disrespecting life by advocating killing the unborn, or promoting a homosexual agenda. Have you? God help us! Under the pretense of "freedom," atrocities are committed and the privilege to speak freely is perverted. The National Organization of Women is only a "front for legalized euthanasia," promoting the killing of innocent unborn babies; and "smut peddlers" exploit the Constitution's First Amendment, with the help of corrupted judges to promote their obscene, vulgar and profane products, and services. God Forgive Us!

CHAPTER TWO:
COMMUNIST AMERICA

So, you do not think that the United States is a Marxist nation. Well, I will present the facts and you decide.

Communist Manifesto, by Marx and Engels states that ten principles must be implemented into a political system to transform a government from capitalism (Free Enterprise) to Communism. By my observation Communism has a resounding victory in the USA. Have a look:

"The Ten Planks of Communism," by Marx and Engels

1. Abolition of property in land and application of all rents of land to public purposes. Anyone who owns land pays property tax. For example, with a property tax rate of 5%, you pay 5% of your property's value each year to the government. If you don't pay property taxes, your land is confiscated, and sold on the court house steps. Effectively, a person doesn't own their land; it's a perpetual transferable lease from the government. Owning something means you don't have to pay anything for the continuing privilege of ownership. By this standard, nobody in the USA owns land. All land is owned by the government and rent is paid. Through tyrannical zoning laws, wetlands regulations, EPA regulations, etc., we no longer control our lands. Our once strong private property rights have been abolished through regulatory oppression, bureaucratic tyranny and unbiblical types of taxation. We are serfs, we own nothing!

2. A heavy progressive or graduated income tax. In 1913, the 16 Amendment to our Constitution was illegally rarified (Read

Bill Benson's book, The Law that Never Was." The government has used this "law" to gain control of our earnings and takes its toll first. If you do not pay, the IRS (a Gestapo agency, or akin to the KBG) will come after you. The law is unconstitutional and oppressive. The tax code is such an obvious tool of social manipulation. Do you think it's any coincidence that the tax code has a marriage penalty, and the number of unmarried couples living together has gone up? One of the stated goals of the is the abolition of the family.

3. Abolition of all right of inheritance. Estate taxes are pretty hefty. People with tremendous wealth can use trusts to dodge estate taxes. However, they're paying an effective tax to their accountants and estate planning lawyers; for large estates, estate planning services take a percent of assets. Estate taxes hit hardest on families with a business valued in the $1M-$10M range. Their business may not have the cash flow to pay the estate taxes and they may be forced to sell. One of the tests of ownership is the ability to grant a thing to another person. If you aren't free to do that, you don't really own anything.

4. Confiscation of the property of all emigrants and rebels. There are many laws making it very easy for the government to confiscate the property of "terrorists" and other criminals. The law makes it very easy for the government to seize assets of people accused of tax evasion. With a globalized economy, you can't really transfer wealth outside of the country. Where else could it go? All countries have the same bad rules for capital ownership, with the USA having slightly better rules! The US has relatively few emigrants, but we have plenty of rebels. While assorted tax resistors and government regulatory resistors fall in the rebel category, the new favorite catch-all prosecutorial group is "suspected" drug dealers. Suspicion is all it takes. No need to worry about due process. This is the drug war. Police Forces can confiscate your entire house if they find one pot leaf in it (and how easy is it for evidence to be planted by the authorities?). The same holds true for your car, or boat. Just having a stack of money that could be used to buy drugs is suspicious.

5. Centralization of credit in the hands of the State, by means of a national bank with State capital and an exclusive monopoly.

Don't think so? Quick, who's Chairman of the Federal Reserve? That's right, our good friend, Ben Bernanke. He and the rest of the board set the prime-lending rate, and control the money supply. In my Keynesian slanted Macro Economics class, they called this "fiscal and monetary policy". After a good dose of Austrian economics, it is "Objective 5 of the Communist Manifesto – Government Command Economy" or "taxation via inflation". Control of the banking system by the fed is so complete that Wall Street, the supposed paragon of free-market capitalism, wags up and down to the mumblings of a single un-elected bureaucrat. The Feds expansion of fiat currency can and will cause our nation to collapse, and the "Sheeple" will cry out for the government to do something! The end to our freedoms is in sight!!

6. Centralization of the means of communication and transport in the hands of the State. There is pretty heavy government regulation of transportation (still in the hands of the state), and communication. Most telecommunication companies are big corporations that are heavily regulated. Centralized control in a few corporations is effectively the same as State control. A government-granted monopoly with heavy regulation is the same as State control. Televisions and newspapers are concentrated in a few corporations. However, the Internet is one noteworthy exception that is at risk, for now, but is in line of being controlled soon, if "network neutrality" is stopped.

7. Extension of factories and instruments of production owned by the State; the bringing into cultivation of waste-lands, and the improvement of the soil generally in accordance with a common plan. The government is taking control of corporations as they see fit and legislation has and is being passed to give the government control of any company it deems is a threat to failure. The farming industry is heavily regulated and government subsidized. Most industrial farms follow the practices set out by a few agricultural companies (i.e. Monsanto). Fewer factories are built in the USA. Besides, concentration of manufacturing power in a few big corporations is effectively the same as State control.

8. Equal liability of all to labour. Establishment of industrial armies, especially for agriculture. I think that "industrial

armies" could be interpreted as huge corporate control of factories and farms. The food industry is certainly heavily regulated, but may mean that the modern form of the industrial army is undeniably the union. Just like an army, unions use force to get their way. Sometimes its physical force, other times political force. Naturally, the unions, consisting of the democratic mob, have passed legislation making it legal for them to organize, but illegal for their employer to terminate them. Forward the communist army! "Equal liability of all to labour," means that most people are employees/wage slaves, rather than entrepreneurs. There are so many barriers to starting a small business that most people are effectively forced to work as employees. The average person is a laborer, not a capital owner. Even a small business owner is effectively a government employee, because of the confiscatory effect of income taxes. Now, with current legislation, the government may set salaries and wages for management or owners of businesses, and certainly can control earnings through taxation

9. Combination of agriculture with manufacturing industries; gradual abolition of the distinction between town and country, by a more equable distribution of the population over the country. Agriculture is mostly industrialized now. Small farmers are mostly out, or marginalized. The increasing power and regulation of the Federal government means that the ability of cities to make their own laws is reduced. For example, people in some states want to legalize marijuana but are forbidden by the Federal enforcement of drug laws. Notice the reference to "equable distribution" of the populace. This can only be accomplished by land redistribution. The communists saw the distinction between city dwellers, townies, and country folk. They knew the city, filled with factory workers, was their natural base from which to mount an assault on the property rights conscious farmers and aristocratic landowners. While moving people into the countryside seems antithetical to today's environmental movement, the two are actually after the same goal: reduction of property rights.

10. Free education for all children in public schools. Abolition of children's factory labour in its present form. Combination of education with industrial production. We've certainly

reached the education camp ideal espoused in the communist manifesto. This is another huge win for Communism. There are huge problems with the current implementation of schools. Even though there are private schools, most of them follow the model set by public schools. They are better in quality, but suffer the same structural defect. The combination of education with industrial production looks exactly like the work to school programs that find such favor with our public education system. The abolition of factory slave labor and the preservation of third world "habitat" are two verses in the same tribal chant of the neo-communist environmental movement. Schools are designed to created obedient workers. Their "loss-avoidance" training means that they are reluctant to risk any sort of job loss, making them obedient workers.

Here are a few more of the Communist Goals, as listed in the January 10, 1963 Congressional Record of the United States, concerning Degeneracy in the Arts and Entertainment.

Continue discrediting American culture by degrading all forms of artistic expression. An American Communist cell was told to 'eliminate all good sculpture from parks and buildings, substitute shapeless, awkward and meaningless forms' (Ten Commandments removed from Judge Moore's courthouse in Alabama).

Control art critics and directors of art museums. Our plan is to promote ugliness, repulsive, meaningless art.

Eliminate all laws governing obscenity by call them 'censorship' and a violation of free speech and free press.

Break down cultural standards of morality by promoting pornography and obscenity in books, magazines, motion pictures, radio, and TV.

Present homosexuality, degeneracy and promiscuity, as 'normal, natural, healthy (alternative) lifestyles. Now, we have legalized homosexual marriage!

Is this what we are now witnessing? You tell me!!

Those who control the media are a taboo topic among the "Talking Heads." In Congress, among evangelicals and mainline conservative talk radio, the subject of who controls the media is never mentioned. It is discussed only on the internet or on far Right alternative talks radio.

This is astonishing, considering that almost every substantial library in America contains a number of books confirming such control. These include Neil Gabler's *An Empire of Their Own: How the Hollywood was Invented,* and Hoberman and Shandler's *Entertaining America. I go into detail in my research papers, which I will send to you free. Just send me an email and request my papers.*

These encyclopedic histories of those who control the American media outdo any efforts by "truth seekers" to document an astonishing, frightening fact: The majority of media news and information to the American public comes from one group of people. This helps explain why the controlled media is so relentlessly anti-Christian, constantly pushing immorality and the liberal, New World Order and Marxist political agenda.

Why are Christians marginalized, made fun of or ridiculed in films and TV? Why is the Palestinian perspective not included in the news? Face the forbidden truth: "the media speaks with a controlled voice." Please do not get the impression that I support terrorist, Palestinians or Jews, I do not, but I don't feel that Palestine gets a fair shake when the news is broadcast. By the way, my grandfather was a Jew. My family name was originally, "Braunschweig." So, do not call me, "anti-Semitic!"

Politicians and others with authoritarian tendencies will never come out and directly say that they want to control your life. They'll tell you to support some piece of legislation in the name of fairness, or the environment, or safety, or I am working for the children, or "our" future, or humanitarian intervention, or national security. How about helping the elder and taking care of your health? Have you heard this before? These hypocrites have one goal and that is to remain in power, and continue in a lavish egotistical life-style.

What you must understand is that we have slipped into a Marxist society, and we will eventually become just another nation in A New World Order. The only "hope" we have is a complete political revolution and throw all the rascals out of office and start with a clean slate; or it may take a bloody revolution led by the military.

Ken Braun

"A ROSE BY ANY OTHER NAME IS STILL A ROSE" ----<u>Marxism by any other name is still "Marxism," even if it's called "a Democracy!"</u>

CHAPTER THREE: MEDIA "TALKING HEADS" EXPOSED FOR WHAT THEY REALLY ARE

Have you ever noticed how the so-called conservative "talking-heads" in the media never mentions who control the media (who heads up the major media corporations), and never discloses the agenda of the Bilderbergs, or other globalist organizations? In fact, if you call-in to one talk shows, and attempt to have a sensible discussion regarding the CFR, Trilateral Commission, or the Round Table, you are immediately cut off or discredited as a conspiracy nut. Why won't Bill O'Reilly or Sean Hannity have a legitimate discussion regarding our fiat currency, the history of the Federal Reserve (the truth), or even some of the controversies surrounding 9/11? These "talking-heads" will call you a "kook," if you even ask questions regarding "unanswered questions" involving the investigation of 9/11. Why?

Well, let take a good look at these so called conservatives and expose their true colors.

<u>Sean Hannity</u>
Hannity is s strong supporter of George Bush. Any true conservative who had done his homework knows that the Bush Family is tied to the Council on Foreign Relations, the Bilderberg Group, and the Trilateral Commission.

Let's start with Grand-paw Bush: Prescott Sheldon Bush was the father of President George H.W. Bush and the grandfather of President George

W. Bush. At one time, he was an unsuccessful Republican candidate for the United States Senate. However in 1950, he obtained a seat in the Senate after the death of Senator James O'Brien. **Prescott Bush was also a Wall Street executive banker with Brown Brothers/Harriman, who were one of the key financiers of Hitler's Nazi regime.**

On October 20, 1942, President Roosevelt signed the "Trading With the Enemy Act_ into law, and the U.S. government ordered the seizure of Nazi German banking operations, under its jurisdiction. Prescott Bush was charged with trading with the enemy, however, other than being charged, he was ever held accountable. Germany based Brown Brothers / Harriman assets in New York were seized. Assets confiscated included, Union Banking Corporation (UBC) (for Thyssen and Brown Brothers Harriman); Holland-American Trading Corporation (with Harriman); Seamless Steel Equipment Corporation (with Harriman); and Silesian-American Corporation (Partially owned by Germans who attempted to take over the company, in response the U.S. government seized German owned minority shares leaving the U.S. partners to carry on the business.)

The Nazi assets sized by the U.S. government were held in safekeeping by the government for the duration of the war then returned to their owners after the war, except for the Germans. Prescott Bush, who was on the board of directors of Union Banking Corporation, was reimbursed $1,500,000. These Nazi war assets were responsible for launching the Bush family fortune.

Manuscripts proving Prescott Bush's Nazi ties can be found in the National Archives and the Library of Congress documenting the business relationship between W. Averell Harriman, George Herbert Walker, and Prescott Bush, who served as U.S. partners of, and private bankers for, Nazi industrialist Fritz Thyssen, the financial architect of The Third Reich.

Does George W. Bush have anything in common with Hitler? You judge!

"I believe that God wants me to be president." - George W. Bush —

"I would like to thank Providence and the Almighty for choosing me of all people to be allowed to wage this battle for Germany" - Hitler - Berlin March, 1936

"God is not on the side of any nation, yet we know He is on the side of justice. Our finest moments [as a nation] have come when we faithfully served the cause of justice for our own citizens, and for the people of other lands." - George W. Bush

"If we pursue this way, if we are decent, industrious, and honest, if we so loyally and truly fulfill our duty, then it is my conviction that in the future as in the past the Lord God will always help us" - Adolf Hitler, at the Harvest Thanksgiving Festival on the Buckeburg held on 3 Oct. 1937

"Freedom and fear, justice and cruelty have always been at war, and we know that God is not neutral between them." - George W. Bush. (This sounds like "Tragedy and Hope;" The "tragedy of war and the hope for peace.")

"Never in these long years have we offered any other prayer but this: Lord, grants to our people peace at home, and grant and preserve to them peace from the foreign foe!" - Hitler - Nuremberg Sept. 13, 1936.

My point is "God is used by politicians when it is to their advantage, and the exploitation of religion and God is not limited to Bush and Hitler. When it is advantageous for politicians to use God or religion for personal gain, they do not hesitate (Just listen to Obama in his speeches regarding "collective salvation")

Are we a Communist nation already, and do not realize it?

On August 24, 1963, Nikita Khrushchev himself remarked in a speech he gave earlier in Yugoslavia, "I once said, 'We will bury you,' and I got into trouble with it. Of course we will not bury you with a shovel. Your own working class will bury you," a reference to the Marxist saying, "The proletariat is the undertaker of capitalism."

The United States is already in its grave, and its only hope is to "rise from the dead," but it must come from those who love freedom and will accept responsibility to restore our Constitution. All of the principles of Marx and Engels that are so well entrenched in our political system must be expunged, but by whom? Certainly the way will not be led by phony talking-head conservative. I have never heard Sean mention "The Ten Planks of Communism," or talk about how our system has slipped into

Marxism. In fact, I have never heard him say that Obama was Marxist, have you?

Sean continues to have Newt Gingrich (one of the "insiders") on his program touting him as a conservative. Well, let me tell you about "Newt the puke."

Gingrich is a member of the CFR, and supported NAFTA, He is totally corrupt. When he was Speaker of the House, nothing "truly" conservative happened. Do not tell me about a balanced budget. A budget is nothing more than numbers, which mean nothing unless extreme control is exercised. Spending increased, our debt increased, abortion remained, no Federal Judges were impeached for treason, and there were no true tax reforms to get rid of the pro-Marxist income tax (now, he wants to appear as a true conservative and advocates a "Fair Tax" – what a phony) … He did nothing to eliminate fiat currency and never once talked about monetary reforms.

Morally, Newt was worse than Clinton; while condemning Bill Clinton for his affairs, Newt was having oral sex with one of his campaign worker (reported in Vanity Fair). Gingrich has been married three times. He married his first wife, Jackie Battley, in 1962, and divorced her in 1981. He informed his wife, Jackie, of his intent to divorce her while she was in the hospital, recuperating from cancer surgery. Gingrich married his second wife, Marianne Ginther, in the fall of 1981. They divorced in 1999, after revealing that he had been having an affair with a House aide, Callista Bisek. Gingrich and Bisek were married the following year. So, do not be fooled by this hypocrite.

Gingrich, who considered running for president in 2008, called for a revival of the Reagan revolution, agreeing with Tom DeLay in characterizing the Obama budget plan as "the boldest effort to create a European socialism we have ever seen." (Translation: THIS IS WHAT IT IS ALL ABOUT –NEWT "NWO" GINGRICH PREPARING TO LEAD CHRISTIANS TO THEIR POLITICAL 'SLAUGHTER" ONCE AGAIN IN 2012, JUST AS IT HAPPENED IN 2008 WITH NEWT'S FELLOW CFR-MEMBER JOHN "McCAIN.]

Watch out for this Presidential ticket for 2012: Globalists Gingrich and Mitt Romney may 'team up' as presidential / vice presidential Republican candidates – do not be surprised, or vice-versa...

When Sean introduces Newt, as Mr. Speaker, I all most "throw-up" thinking how Gingrich supported legislation, politicians, programs and treaties which furthered the agenda of the CFR. Now, Newt wants to take a conservative stance and support a Fair Tax......what was he thinking when he was Speaker of The House? He had a chance to introduce true tax reforms (not the liberal Reagan kind) and monetary reforms?

Sean has already shown his true colors.

Sean also has Oliver North as a guest. North should have been tried for treason, in my opinion and arrested for drug running, and money laundering. There's been documented evidence that it was George Bush and Oliver North and the CIA that was bringing in the narcotics into Mena, Arkansas (already discussed). I am not sure that the CIA is not still involved in narcotics; after all, Afghanistan is the number one opium producer in the world and the trade brings in billions to global banks.

What is being done about it? Nothing!!

North and Clinton needs to answer, under oath, their involvement with Barry Seal (as well as Bush), and drug dealer Dan Lassiter (whom Clinton pardoned before leaving office). Prove me wrong!

Sean supports pseudo-conservatives, such as the one already mention as well as others (Cheney, Rove, Romney, etc., etc.). He could not stand the thoughts of Ron Paul winning any polls or getting any creditable recognition during the 2008 election primaries. Hannity is a neo-con fake conservative, and is a dangerous talking head representing the establishment; knowingly or unknowingly.

Glenn Beck

Ah, Mr. Chalk Board and self proclaimed authority on history and the Constitution; however, Beck is almost as bad as Hannity. Beck praise of Calvin Coolidge indicates that to me that he is just another phony attempting to fool true conservatives. Coolidge was a Progressive, and well accepted by the International-financial coterie (The "Power Elite" – Quigley referred to these "want to be masters of the world," as the International-financial coterie). Beck position of favoring a flat tax on income proves that he supports the government's control of our earning (our property), which is absolutely a Marxist principle (go back and read plank #2 in "The Ten Planks of Communism).

Becks talks about God and Christianity, but does he really believe that Jesus is our Lord and Savior, and was born of virgin birth? Ask him!! A Christian is a person who believes that Christ is Lord.

Now, Beck tells the "Tea Party Movement" it should follow the example of Martin Luther King, Jr. Anyone studying the life of King knows damn well he was not so reverend. This whore-monger was a Communist. King learned how to create civil disorder at the Highlander Folk School. (FBI Report: The Highlander Folk School, located in Monteagle, TN, was founded by Don West, District Director of the Communist Party in North Carolina, and Miles Norton, Director of the Commonwealth College. Based upon testimony by members of the school, the school was cited for conducting subversive activities by the State of Tennessee, and closed by court order in 1960). King's key advisors were Communist and King once admitted to the author who assisted King in writing King's autobiography that he was a Marxist...

My comments about Martin Luther King, Jr. are not to degrade his name, as the records will do this once they are "un-sealed," but to expose the truth, which Glenn Beck will not do. By praising King, Beck may be patronizing blacks to gain their acceptance, and support. What Beck is doing could be good for him, as it may ease the distrust and conflict between races, and maybe, a lie is better than the truth to accomplish this goal. However, I am not concern with patronizing anyone, but about the truth in King's life and his motives. Nor am I fooled into thinking that we are all basically "the same," I realize there are differences between races, religions, and cultures, and what I feel is needed is for all the people to recognize these differences, and find common ground to live and work together, to expel, and destroy the agenda of the PE and restore dignity and freedoms to all men, under God that provides equality of our Constitutional rights.

Martin Luther King, Jr., is another public figure that was assassinated for the martyr effect. As the evidence below shows King's corruption, womanizing and Communist sympathies was becoming more a liability to the Civil Rights agenda than an asset. It was only a matter of time before King's reputation would self-destruct. By carefully conspiring and planning his death and blaming it on a supposed racist, the "Powers That Be" could turn MLK into a hero. With the assistance of controlled judges, a controlled media, and a controlled political system, "The Establishment" was able to have his records sealed and make sure the public would not have access to the real Martin Luther King. These records are still sealed.

The evidence of wrongdoing by King is really taboo, and a well kept secret; colluding judges sealed the evidence for 50+ years in official archives to make sure that by the time the public finds out about it, all the guilty parties will be out of office or dead. This is precisely why the files on Martin Luther King were sealed. This was done while politicians debated on whether King would be worthy to be honored by declaring his birthday as national holiday. According to a former Asst. Director of the FBI, who had first-hand knowledge of the facts, 14 of the 15 file cabinets are filled with surveillance files documenting King's chronic pornography and prostitution habits, including his raunchy activities while in Sweden accepting his Nobel Prize, which would have been made public had the files been left open for public scrutiny. The other file cabinet, full of evidence, traced his connection to Marxist. Had the public known of this information, King would have been disgraced rather than honored. What we need is a piece of legislation making it a crime to classify, as secret, any evidence of a crime, by government officers or agent. But then again, as long as only government insiders are allowed to view and judge the contents of classified material, the public will never know the truth--except through a leak by some patriotic government employee.

There is a famous picture taken the day before King's assassination featuring Hosea Williams, Jesse Jackson, Martin Luther King Jr., and Ralph David Abernathy on the balcony of the Lorraine Motel Memphis hotel; April 3, 1968. The picture has been shown millions of times; King, the day before his death, greeting his supporters. What is not publicly known is what happened the night before his death. Newsweek magazine from January 19, 1998 gives you a small glimpse of the real Martin Luther King Jr. Do not take my word for it, see the following proof "Pillar of Fire: America, in the King Years," 1963-65.

(Book reviews) Jon Meacha 01/19/98 Newsweek, Page 62 - January 6, 1964, was a long day for Martin Luther King Jr. He spent the morning seated in the reserved section of the Supreme Court, **listening as lawyers argued New York Times Co. v. Sullivan, a landmark case rising out of** King's crusade against segregation in Alabama. The minister was something of an honored guest: Justice Arthur Goldberg quietly sent down a copy of Kings Account of the Montgomery bus boycott, "Stride toward Freedom," asking for an autograph (how corrupt are Supreme Court appointees? You be the judge). That night King retired to his room at the Willard Hotel. There FBI bugs reportedly picked up 14 hours of party chatter, the clinking of glasses and the sounds of illicit sex--including King's cries of "I'm f--ing for God" and "I'm not a Negro tonight!"

Note: What is not mentioned in this article is that Martin Luther King was having sex with three White women, one of whom he brutally beat while screaming the above mentioned quotes. Much of the public information on King's use of church money to hire prostitutes and his beating them came from King's close personal friend, Rev. Ralph Abernathy (pictured above), in his 1989 book, "And the walls came tumbling down."

Sources:
Newsweek Magazine 1-19-1998, page 62

This is the man Beck wants us to follow as an example?
The Civil Rights issue, itself, was a charade of a misguided march for equality. I guess it depends on how one defines equality as to whether or not we all are now equal. Certainly, one can make an argument that for the majority of blacks, condition are worse now than before the Civil Right Acts were passed by congress and signed by the President; as the percentage of unwed mothers and fatherless families has increased for blacks, and jobless blacks, especially, for the younger ones, has increased. For whites, conditions are worse in the educational system, since Brown V The Board of Education. Our system has been dummied down. Did this happen because of forced integration and busing? Again, you be the judge. Also, the crime rate has increased, and the races are more divided, but it is subtle. We are constantly hearing about racism, as we witness blacks exploiting blacks, claiming injustices still exist and creating an atmosphere of hate; i.e., Sharpton and Jackson.

If Beck wants a black person to acknowledge as an example to follow, he should consider, "Alan Keyes," While I do not agree with Keyes on all issues, he is the only black member of the "cultist elitist" that stands for some of the moral and Constitutional principles on which our nation was founded. Keyes has also celebrated the life of MLK, Jr.; however, I personally feel that Keyes knows the truth about King, but for the sake of not offending many naïve and uninformed black, he is willing to allow the truth to be distorted. This may be his position, as to avoid destruction of modern history's only black icon, up until Obama (it will be interesting to see how history portrays Obama). In reality, what King did was destructive to both blacks and whites, and very divisive.

To learn more about King, send me your email address, and I will provide the proof supporting my views and position.

Beck pleads with member of the Tea Party to follow, King, who was a Marxist, and Beck says he is a patriot??? Something is wrong with this picture. Then Beck has a female author on his "show" who wrote a book about Coolidge. She is a member of the CFR and Beck mentioned in his introduction of her that "she is a member of that evil organization, the CFR (paraphrased)." He said it in a way to make it seem that anyone knowing the real truth of how "evil" the CFR really is, must be some kind of a conspiracy nut. Beck is a tool, a stooge, knowingly or unknowingly for the PE. Ask Beck who control the media and why issues like Agenda 21 are never exposed (which you can find in my research that I will send free of charge to anyone interested)? His actions proves to me that by portraying a member of the CFR as a conservative, and a non-progressive, he is a hypocrite; Becks words diminishes the truth about the destructive agenda of this organization. More overly, when Beck speaks of the Illuminati, the Masons, or any other organization claimed by many to be tied to a movement promoting a one world government, he sort of snickers and make fun of anyone who disagrees that history happens by accident. If a "caller or guest" attempts to give evidence that there are those in history who scheme to control its outcome, they are insulted, discredited, and embarrassed. It is my opinion that Beck plays a role, portraying himself as a regular person with conservative views, while in truth, he is a person filled with just enough truth to convince people that he is a conservative, but I feel he is part of a scheme to control what news conservatives hear. Is it possible that Beck may be a "plant" for the establishment to mislead true conservatives with half-truths and false information, to discredit anyone with the absolute truth which will expose the Establishment's plan to move our nation into the New World Order, and to keep us from interfering with the true agenda of the Elitist? I do not know; I just "judge a tree by its fruits."

Still think Beck is one of us?

Rush Limbaugh

I have sent Rush Limbaugh two emails regarding his position on several issues, but have not received a reply. I probably will not hear from him. One message this I sent was regarding his theory on events in history (does he think that all events occur by accident?) and the other email was regarding, global organizations, and the positions, actions, and policies (both personal and political) of certain individuals who call themselves conservatives.

Rush Limbaugh, was born January12, 1951, into a prominent Missouri family, and raised in a town about thirty miles from the Kentucky border. His grandfather, the first Rush Hudson Limbaugh, was America's Ambassador to India in the Eisenhower administration (which may explain many of Limbaugh's Neo Con views). His uncle, Stephen Limbaugh, was appointed a Federal Judge by Ronald Reagan (another pseudo-conservative), and his cousin, Stephen Limbaugh, Jr., who was appointed to the U.S. District Court by George W. Bush; were politically active and part of the establishment. His father was a local attorney, who imbued his children with what many consider "pseudo-conservative ideology." His brother, David Limbaugh, is a lawyer and "conservative writer."

Limbaugh claims to backs many "traditional conservative" causes with some exceptions -- he supports capital punishment, opposes abortion, claims that global warming is a lie, etc.; etc. These views certainly give the perception that he is a true conservative, but is he really? Callers are pre-screened; few who disagree with the host are allowed on the air, especially, those who have concerns with "The New World Order," and global organizations. Limbaugh will quickly intimidate anyone bringing up the subject of a "conspiracy." Those who cannot be intimidated or who are well informed are quickly "cut off the air." He is very intelligent and spends most of his air time blasting away at Democrats. Rarely, will you hear him adversely criticize a Republican, unless it is one that holds the views similar to those of Ron Paul; that is, until recently. Thanks to the Internet, people are becoming better informed and when "talking heads" have guest like Scott Brown, or tout his so called conservative views, these informed individuals will take issue with these so call conservative "mouth pieces," and expose their lies.

"In his book *The Way Things Ought to Be*, Limbaugh wrote, "I believe that strong, wholesome family values are at the very core of a productive, prosperous, and peaceful society." I do not know how he defines "peaceful," or "productive," but I am sure he has his own Neo Con definition. Regarding his "family values," what are 'Limbaugh's family values?' His first wife, Roxy Maxine McNeely, was a sales secretary at a Kansas City radio station, as I found by searching the Internet. She was granted divorce under grounds of "incompatibility" after almost three years of marriage (maybe, she really thought Rush was a conservative, but found out differently, after they were married). His second wife, Michelle Sixta, was an usherette, at the Royals' ball park; and a college student. They divorced after about five years. He met his third wife, aerobics instructor Marta Fitzgerald, through CompuServe's dating service, and Supreme Court Justice <u>Clarence Thomas</u> performed their wedding ceremony. According to the *Palm Beach Post*, Limbaugh and Fitzgerald maintained separate houses during their marriage. She divorced Limbaugh at his request after ten years of marriage, at about the time Limbaugh began dating then-CNN anchor <u>Daryn Kagan</u> (I do not know who he is with at the present time)." (From: nndb.com/people/428/000022362/)---So much for his high moral standards, and family values. Seem that Newt Gingrich and Rush have a lot in common, when it comes to women, and sexual behavior.

Limbaugh is the epitome of a hypocrite; he reaches ordinary folks, because he sounds like "Joe the Plumber." (While he complains about the wealthy elite who controls America: "All of these rich guys -- like the Kennedy family, Soros, and Perot; you will not hear him mention Bush, Cheney, or other global elitists). He is milking hundreds of millions from his network of radio stations and sponsors because naïve listeners are convinced that Rush represents them and the conservative movement. This is far from the truth.

It is my opinion that Limbaugh, Hannity and O'Reilly and the other Republican Party "talking-head hacks" are, in reality, pseudo-conservatives. O'Reilly portrays himself as an independent, but in reality, he is just another FOX News, "talking-head" that gives just enough credit to others point of view to appear "fair and balanced;" but only up to a point. O'Reilly and the others defend nation building, wars in the Middle East, and "Neo-Con politics," while ignoring the so-called terrorist from Saudi Arabia, fiat currency, the illegal progressive income tax, the FED destructive policies, and semi-open borders; or simply, ignore any issues, which does not fit the agenda of the "Neo-Con, pseudo-conservative establishment" (this is not truthful nor is it fair and balance - not in the least). A true conservative, or patriot, supports protection of our borders (and deporting all illegal's aliens), actually "cuts" in government spending (not just a balanced budget, which can be achieved by manipulating numbers), true tax reforms (get rid of the Pro-Marxist income tax and the IRS); monetary reforms that eliminates fiat currency and the FED; and stop the expansions of "an empire," by fighting useless and winless wars; and occupying other countries with our military. A true patriot would deny support for any incumbent that has served more than six years, with the exception of a very few, and would speak out against political appointees to the Supreme Court. A true conservative would demand term limits (but only if it can be done without weakening the Constitution – must be concerned with a Constitutional Convention), and support third party candidates against liberal republican. A true patriot would demand that tax paid retirement plans for elected officials and their appointees be eliminated. --------*"By their fruits, ye shall know them."*

It's truly amazing how Limbaugh has been playing this "liberal" vs. "conservative" shtick for thirty years, but when it comes to real conservatives, such as Ron Paul, Limbaugh has a condescending attitude toward their views. In fact, he is downright insulting; while supporting pseudo-conservatives; such as Bush, Gingrich, Reagan, and others.

Personally, I feel that Limbaugh is the greatest of all phony conservatives, and would appreciate answers to the questions I emailed to him to verify his true position – conservative, liberal, or pseudo-conservative?

All the talking heads that most of us listen to, and watch on FOX are Neo-Con pseudo-conservative, this includes Laura, Ann, Mike Reagan, and Bill O'Reilly (claims he is not a conservative or liberal- well, maybe, he is right, maybe he is a promoter of the establishment's NWO, as they all have the same boss!)

On February 18, 2009, in an interview that discussed, in part, the confiscation of legally-owned guns during a declared state of emergency (as was the case in the aftermath of Hurricane Katrina), O'Reilly affirmed his support of such confiscations. This guy is a former History teacher? It was explained to O'Reilly that whether or not there's a state of emergency, it's still unconstitutional to confiscate lawfully-owned guns from honest citizens wanting to defend themselves, the FOX talking head retorts, "That's a pretty extreme position." Extreme position? Has he never read the Constitution – a history teacher??? For most law-abiding Americans, the notion that the government can suspend the Constitution is a threat to our freedoms.

Anyone that has followed the antics of Bill O'Reilly for any appreciable amount of time knows, at best, he is a Neo Con, not a true Conservative or Liberal. I won't bother going into all the various positions he has held over time that convinces me that he is a real phony. If you want the truth about O'Reilly, please contact me and I will send you my research on him, FREE!

He did his best to justify the war with Iraq, and still defends his position with "the world is a better place without Saddam Hussein," as does Sean, but let me remind you that Saddam was an ally to the United States, and fought an eight year war against Iran (a member of the evil axis empire). I was in Iraq, twice, after the first Persian Gulf War, and I it was the only Muslim country that I found that allowed Christian Churches inside the country. In fact, Saddam had Christians as members of his Cabinet. If you want to know the truth about why war was declared on Iraq, please request my research for this book. It is free (braunkenh@aol.com. Saddam was set up!!

The media is controlled, and we are fed propaganda 24/7. The entertainment business is also controlled by the same "Elitist," with an agenda to change our nations from sovereignty to one of "dependence and a collective system."

All one has to do these days is turn on the television to see the cesspool that is loosely called "Entertainment." The movies and the stage are no better. Everything is contaminated with the stench of "Raunchy! Sex! Violence! Pornography! And Propaganda!! A typical example is Jerry Springer, and the smut comedy network, along with MTV and other so called music stations. The Entertainment industry is controlled by those with the same plan to destroy our morals and eventually our nation, including many of the actors. You must read Marx and Engels!!

I will be delighted to provide a list of those who control the media, universities, and major financial institutions -upon request – just email me!

CHAPTER FOUR:
RELIGIOUS CHARLETONS
LEADING RELIGIOUS SHEEPLE

"DO NOT BELIEVE EVERYONE WHO CLAIMS TO SPEAK BY THE SPIRIT. You must TEST THEM to see if the spirit they have comes from God. For there are many FALSE PROPHETS in the world. This is how we know if they have the Spirit of God: If a person claiming to be a PROPHET acknowledges that Jesus Christ came in a real body, that person has the Spirit of God. But if someone claims to be a PROPHET and does not acknowledge the truth about Jesus, that person is NOT from God. Such a person has the spirit of the Antichrist, which you heard is coming into the world and indeed is already here. But you belong to God, my dear children. You have already won a victory over those people, because the Spirit who lives in you is greater than the spirit who lives in the world. THOSE PEOPLE BELONG TO THIS WORLD, SO THEY SPEAK FROM THE WORLD VIEWPOINT, AND THE WORLD LISTENS TO THEM. But we belong to God, and those who know God listens to us. If they do not belong to God, they do not listen to us. That is how we know if someone has the Spirit of Truth or the SPIRIT OF DECEPTION." ---1 John 4:1-6

The following are some of the lyrics from Joe South's, "The Games People Play." I feel that these words best describe today's religious charlatans:

"Now look here
People walking up to you
Singing glory hallelujah (ha-ha)
And they're tryin' to sock it to you

In the name of the Lord
They're gonna teach you how to meditate
Read your horoscope, cheat your faith
And further more to hell with hate
Come on; get on board, whoa-ah
- Chorus -
Now wait a minute
Look around tell me what you see
What's happening to you and me?
God grant me the serenity
To just remember who I am, whoa-ah
'Cause you've given up your sanity
For your pride and your vanity
Turn your back on humanity
Oh, and you don't give a da, da da, da da"

I will confess up front that I am a Christian and a believer that Jesus Christ is Lord and my Savior. I was first baptized in the Baptist Church, and then again in the Church of Christ. However, I have attended many churches, and studied religions of many faiths, I have read excerpts of the Quran, the Talmud; and have some exposure to Eastern religions. I have also studied atheism, and Gnosticism. I have read Darwin's theories, Christopher Hitchens, Richard Dawkins, and Carl Sagan. I viewed and listened very carefully to the debate at Stanford between Jay Richards, and Christopher Hitchens, and I have spent many hours reading books on top of books about evolution and creation. I determined through research and debate that Christianity and creation are the most logic explanation for the existence of man, the universe, and life. I did not come to a conclusion that Christ was my Lord, or that there is a God, or to believe what I believe because of an emotional experience, but through logic and research. My conviction is not due to the preaching by "TV preachers," or some charismatic character standing in a pulpit, asking for money to further his lifestyle. My beliefs, as I stated, are based on my research and logic.

The fact is that charismatic preachers and TV evangelist almost convince me to turn from God and become an agnostic. Had it not been for author Bert Thompson and other like him, I would not have been convinced that there is a God and that Christ is Lord.

What is dangerous about any religion, including Christianity, and atheism, are those who proclaim to know the truth and teach views to fit an agenda that provides them with a standard of living far above that of their congregation, or audiences. Some of these characters are very charismatic and are so suave, and articulate that they are able to convince "the sheeple" there is a need for their services whether it is teaching God, or, for atheist, the non existence of God. Most follow blindly because most people feel that they are not intelligent enough to learn on their own; and need a "more intelligent person" to teach them; or most are not as well educated in theology, or atheism to have confidence in their conviction. They need someone to tell them what they should believe or accept as the truth. Therefore, these "preachers/teachers" have created a need for their services; these charlatans are great salesmen, or just really good con-artist. People will usually give way to those who are able to articulate views convincingly, and are better educated, out of fear of being intimidated. Most people are looking for truth and attempt to find it from those they perceive to be more knowledgeable. When, in reality, religious preachers and/or atheist teachers are not necessarily any smarter than the average person, and are really not needed for anyone to determine his/her own truths; which one can do just by reading.

Who are these "religious phony shepherds" that leads the *"sheeple?" Let's start with one of my favorites (the atheist are named above):*

Kenneth Copeland

Kenneth Copeland started his ministry under Oral Roberts (now diseased, but Roberts' son has stepped into his father's shoes – "like father, like son"). Copeland was a pilot for Roberts. He and his wife, Gloria are charismatic preachers espousing their **"*name it and claim it preaching*** all seem to adhere to the same philosophy, as Robert's, and to extract money from their followers (and are willing "to take the last crumb for a widow's table"). They teach that you can become a "little god;" and you are able to proclaim your own health and wealth just by speaking it. These two preach that Jesus did not pay for our sins on the cross, but instead went to hell for our atonement. They also say that good health and money comes from our faith in God and if your lack of faith is the reason you are not wealthy and/or healthy; ah, but, you must "plant financial seeds," i.e., give them money).

Walter Martin of the Christian Research Institute said the following:

"The study of the Kingdom of the Cults has taught me many profitable lessons, and this is one of them--error begets error; heresy begets heresy and always in the name of truth, always in the name of the gospel. Those who propagate these erroneous views ('little gods,' the 'born again Jesus,' and so on) have sadly crossed over into the kingdom of the cults and stand in need of genuine repentance, lest they come under the inevitability of divine judgment. It is dangerous, in the presence of God, to affirm oneself as a deity--even with a small 'g.' it is blasphemous to speak in the name of God and utter false prophecies. It is the height of theological folly to reduce God the Son, second Person of the holy Trinity, to a lost sinner with the nature of Satan and then send Him to hell with the requirement of regencration before He can complete the work of redemption." *(Walter Martin, "You Shall Be As Gods," Agony of Deceit, page 92-93)*

The Copeland's, like many TV Preachers, seem to have an agenda, and that is to live a lifestyle of the rich and famous. They are very charming, and can deliver a message so convincing that millions of people are fooled about the truth. Money flows into their coffers and Copeland is not bashful about asking for money, and uses Jesus as an example of why he is entitled to the millions he rakes in: **"It takes money to preach the gospel. Jesus Himself knew that, and contrary to what some people think, His ministry was not a poor one. He had so much money coming in and going out through His ministry that He had to appoint a treasurer. His name was Judas."** *(Kenneth Copeland, "From Faith to Faith A Daily Guide to Victory," December 5)*

Kenneth Copeland Ministries should be investigated for failing to fly disaster relief supplies to Haiti's earthquake victims after allegedly promising aviation assistance during the crises. The international organization, which is also under scrutiny by the Senate Finance Committee for possible abuse of its nonprofit status, has been accused of "unfulfilled" pledges and unaccounted donations. Copeland is a "con artist fraud," in my opinion.

Benny Hinn

The most disgusting of the *religious parasites* is Benny Hinn. His financial "religious" empire scams approximately $200 million a year from unsuspected and naïve Christians, who want to believe that Hinn posses a gift of healing from God.

This "scam-artist" had the audacity and egotistical courage to go live on Larry King and promote his "religious" fraud on national TV. Even now, after he has been exposed as a phony, people still flock to his "so called crusades." What is wrong with you folks? These sheeple who follows and believes Benny Hinn has a gift from God will surely be "sheared of their money." Hinn's self-serving "so called ministry" continues to grow and he continues to appear on TV with his phony "dog and pony show." Under freedom of speech and religious freedoms, he is allowed to extort millions from innocent victims. **Here, again, the Constitution is used against an unsuspecting public; only, this time by so called Christians, to fill their own pockets with lots of money!!**

_Special note: *There's a darker side to Hinn and his organization. In 1998 two members of his inner circle died of heroin overdoses. I would not be surprise that Hinn, himself is not a drug user. In 1999, after one of his many vows of reform, he fired several board members and hired an ex-cop named Mario C. Licciardello to do an internal investigation of his ministry. Licciardello was the brother-in-law of Carman, the popular Christian singer, so many think Hinn considered him "safe." But Licciardello did such a good job – taking hundreds of depositions and getting to the bottom of the heroin use – that Hinn then sued him. This should tell you something. Did Mario get too close to the truth? While Licciardello was still his head of security, the ministry filed a lawsuit demanding that all his files be turned over and sealed, because their public release could result in the end of the ministry. One day before Hinn was supposed to give his deposition in this case; Licciardello had a mysterious heart attack and died. The Hinn organization made an out-of-court settlement with Licciardello's widow, which included sealing the court papers. How corrupt is the Hinn organization? Now, we may find out more about this charlatan from his ex-wife who filed for divorce. In February, 2010, Suzanne Hinn filed divorce papers against Benny Hinn in Orange County (California) Superior Court, citing irreconcilable differences. The Hinns separated on Jan. 26 and Benny Hinn has moved out and is living in Dana Point, a wealthy coastal community in southern Orange County. However, his wife will probably remain silent due to the money she will receive from Hinn in the settlement and the money which will continue to flow from his "so called ministry." However, I hope she will "spill the beans" on this fraudulent con-artist.*

Rick Warren and others

The following are direct quotes made by Joseph Farah: "Mega Pastor Rick Warren admits he's in the CFR" —Exclusive WND. Commentary—

WASHINGTON – Rick Warren, the superstar mega-church pastor and bestselling author of "The Purpose Driven Life," had a Damascus Road experience last week – and like Saul of Tarsus, one of the after-effects appears to be blindness

According to the evidence Farah presents in his Internet Post of November 20, 2006, Warren said, "In fact," Warren added, "as a member of the Council on Foreign Relations and Oxford Analytica, I might know as much about the Middle East as you."

It is my opinion that Rick Warren is a "false teacher of the Bible." The CFR's goal is to subvert Christianity, destroy America's sovereignty, destroy traditional family values and deceive the masses into joining a One World, New Age, false religion, i.e., "The New World Order." Too many people search for a spiritual "quick fix." They are fooled into thinking that high profiled preachers are creditable when teaching the Bible. Here is a quick look at one of Warren's most disturbing statements, and I quote, "I apologized to my homosexual friends for making comments in support of California's Proposition-8 (a same-sex marriage ban)." Does Rick sound like a "true follower of Christ" to you? Instead of taking a Biblical stand against homosexuality, Warren apologizes to his homosexual "friends." This is apostasy! Rick Warren is a phony, who knows not the God of the Bible.

He teaches false doctrine and poses as a conservative, as does John Hagee, another phony, who has stated publicly that Jews don't need to be born again because they're special. Well, Jesus told Nicodemus, a Jewish leader, that he would burn in Hell if he didn't get born again. The Jewish people, will "burn in Hell" as quick as any Gentile who rejects Jesus as Lord. John Land is another to beware of. "Dr. Richard Land, President of the Southern Baptists' Ethics and Religious Liberty Commission, was chosen by the CFR elite for promotion after he proved to the Illuminati his base loyalty in two very key areas: (1) Zionism; and (2) Environmentalism. Richard Land, supposedly a religious conservative, strangely is a globalist associate of Jim Wallis, liberal darling and head of the Masonic-oriented *Sojourners* group.

"Land is also an ardent Zionist and is joint backer with Falwell, Hagee, Vines and others, of Jewish and Israeli racist Supremacist."

He is the evangelicals' leading point man on environmentalism. Land essentially teaches that Jesus died on the cross to save Mother Earth *and* to save human souls. Land says that the Great Commission includes the preaching of environmentalism just as much as it does the traditional John 3:16 messages!--------------------

The new gospel of CFR and its evangelical associates holds that *"All Things Are One."* Therefore, the Lord's Prayer, as quoted from the New Age Bible version, *The Message*, as found in Rick Warren's books, uses the well-known occultist phrase, *"as above, so below."* In the King James, we find a quite different rendition, the wording, *"Thy Kingdom come. Thy Will be done in earth, as it is in heaven."*

Every student of the occult instantly recognizes the motto, "as above, so below." This ancient occult formulation, taught from the days of the Egyptian/Greek god, Hermes, brings with it the doctrine that all things are One, that there is no God outside of us, that heaven and earth are now and have always been a unity, and that we, ourselves, are collectively "God." The earth is God, the stars are God, and nature is God. All is one. All is Divine.

Of course, this is pantheism; it is classic Hinduism and New Age. This new gospel is of paramount significance to the Illuminati for it dethrones the external God. The new theology unites all deities and faiths. It refutes any conception of a separate heaven and hell. It sacrileges and deifies planet earth, and it enthrones Man as God incarnate.

It is essentially the old lie spoken of in the Bible's book of *Genesis*, in which Lucifer promised a rebellious Adam and Eve, *"Ye shall be as gods."* It is the lie prophesied in 2nd Thessalonians 2 to come to fullness in these last days, the lie in which the whole world will believe and be damned. It is the lie which is described by the Apostle Paul as the Strong Delusion. This lie represents the Great Apostasy, the falling away that was prophesied." (From a post on the Internet)

The following is a quick look at others:

T.D. Jakes denies the Trinity. That makes his church a cult. Jakes has many other false teachings including word-faith, and the prosperity gospel. He is almost at the top of religious con-artist.

Robert Schuller (*probably the number two phony*) is a positive thinking guru who denies essential Christian doctrine.

Marilyn Hickey is a word-faith teacher teaching false doctrine. One of her tapes records her having a conversation with her billfold, commanding the billfold to fill itself with greenbacks.

Paul Crouch is responsible for an unending open door welcoming false teachers and prophets to his pulpit no matter how outlandish their aberrant teachings may be. Croch has publicly stated that anyone who tests the teaching of any ministers on his programs will go straight to hell. Crouch has openly stated his desire to kill Christian apologists who point out heresy preached on his stations.

Rod Parsley is a word-faith preacher who specializes in whipping up his audiences into altered states of consciousness. His outlandish style is attractive to people who get emotionally carried away by repetitive music and mantras.

R.W. Shambach is an incredible con-artist used by CBN to raise money during their telethons. With scare tactics and false teaching, Shambach surgically convinces thousands to send their money to finance the heretical TBN .

Carlton Pearson has even been attacked by false teachers like T.D. Jakes for his support of the "doctrine of exclusion." This doctrine tries to reconcile Christianity and Islam, claiming the 2 religions is completely compatible.

John Avanzinni is a name-it-and-claim-it mega-star used by TBN whenever they want to promote the hundredfold blessing. Avanzinni also promotes the heresy that God's reason for creating humanity is to duplicate himself.

Kenneth & Gloria Copeland (already covered once) have one of the largest false ministries and influences in America. Copeland teaches that Adam was an exact duplicate of God. Copeland teaches that Jesus became a demonic being when he was crucified and had to go to hell and be

<u>born again</u>. The Copeland's attempt to specialize in word-faith teaching. Copeland calls God, the biggest loser in the Bible, and says Jesus was not God during his earthly life.

John Hagee calls Covenant Theologians heretics, because they do not make a distinction between the church and Israel in the New Testament. Branding them as the "carriers of Hitler's anointing", Hagee divides the body of Christ on secondary issues. Hagee is also extremely dogmatic in his eschatology, failing to understand that there are many diverse interpretations acceptable within the pale of orthodoxy.

Jessie Duplantis' ministry is riddled with errors. Presenting his messages with humor, Duplantis is a typical word-faith clone of Ken Copeland, often preaching from Copeland's pulpit.

Oral Roberts (now deceased) and sons, Richard Roberts are both word-faith con-artists. Oral is the originator of the seed-faith doctrine. Have a need? Plant a seed. Large amounts of cash make the best seed for planting. Both men practice cultic doctrines of bringing their cohorts into altered states of consciousness. I think of Roberts as a money grabbing con-artist, who would take the crumbs off the table of widows and orphans to buy a Cadillac.

Source of the foregoing: "The Internet"

Ted Haggard (and comments on others, including Catholic Priest)

There is a problem in our churches with so-called "men of God." The evangelical church movement as well as the Catholic Church has been plagued with pedophiles and homosexuals. All churches have experienced immoral behavior with it ministers, even in the Church of Christ. We have seen up and coming ministers, such as Skip Stewart in Huntsville, Alabama at the Madison Road Church of Christ, in the 70's, with an adulterous relationship with a married lady in the Church; Skip was also married. Later, a scandal in Franklin, Tennessee with Eddie Miller, Church of Christ minister who had a history of extramarital affairs for years, before being exposed and divorced by his wife; However, the Ted Haggard's homosexual sex scandal that caused his downfall extended to a young male church volunteer who Ted reported having a sexual relationship with the man came forward to church officials in late 2006 shortly after a Denver male prostitute claimed to have had a three-year cash-for-sex relationship with Haggard. It is obvious that Ted is bisexual. What we do not know is how many others did Ted engage in a homosexual relationship with during his ministry when he was suppose to be teaching the Bible and setting an example of a Christ like life?

This immoral life style was made possible because of Ted's power and money. In the case of Catholic Priest, I personally believe that it is mischaracterized as a problem with pedophiles, but rather, their problem, too, is one with homosexuals. There is not one case that I have heard about that involves a girl, and most incidents, the sexual acts were with boys who had reached the age of puberty among the sex scandals in the Catholic Church.

In the Haggard case, the Associated Press reported that an "overwhelming pool of evidence" pointed to an "inappropriate, consensual sexual relationship" that "went on for a long period of time ... it wasn't a one-time act," as Teddy first claimed.

In early 2007, New Life Church disclosed that an investigation uncovered new evidence that Haggard engaged in "sordid conversation" and "improper relationships" - but didn't go into detail. Earlier, a church board member had said there was no evidence that Haggard had sexual relations with anyone but Mike Jones, the former male prostitute.

Haggard confessed to undisclosed "sexual immorality" after Jones' allegations and resigned as president of the National Association of Evangelicals and from New Life Church, where he faced being fired. Notice how, when caught these rascals always confess and asked forgiveness. Without judging their souls, I can certainly judge their behavior and point out that it is not until they are exposed that they suddenly realize their sins and confess.

Jim Bakker

Though he once said he would never start another Christian TV ministry, televangelist Jim Bakker is back on the air. "The New Jim Bakker Show" debuted 16 years to the day of his last broadcast of the "PTL Club," the flagship of a ministry empire that crashed amid headlines about financial and sexual scandal, and saw its head "pseudo-Christian Leader" jailed for five years.

Bakker's new show is taped in middle of the "Bible Belt," Branson, Missouri. Guests since the launch of his constant "soap selling infomercial" begin airing have included Rex Humbard (another charlatan), Tony Orlando and Gary Smalley.

Today, the talk-show program Bakker hosts with his second wife, Lori, is broadcast daily on many TV stations, over 200 cable outlets and internationally through TCT Satellite Network of Worldwide Satellites.

When Bakker told CNN interviewer Larry King shortly after his release in 1994 -- the original sentence having been reduced -- that he would not do television again, "I meant what I said," Bakker said. "When you put your hand in a fire and get burned, the body reacts to that, and it remembers that. What I had been through had been so painful that I could not imagine doing it again." Well, Bakker has changed the definition of never and is back "hustling Christians."

He added: "For years I set about to do a number of other things, but I could not get away from what I feel God called me to do, anointed me to do, and that's Christian television." Blame God or give Him credit, that's Jimmy's reason or excuse for returning to the "air waves."

"The New Jim Bakker Show" has been made possible largely due to one benefactor whose marriage was healed at Heritage USA -- Bakker's former Christian resort -- years ago. Dee and Jerry Crawford own the studio-café, the small hotel across the street and the home where the Bakkers were living.

Up until 1987, televangelist Jim Bakker and his, the wife, wife Tammy Faye were living in extravagance. The way they told it, prosperity was a gift from God, and He had blessed them with an army of followers and immense personal fortunes. The PTL ministry had a "burn rate" of $500,000 per day. Everything seemed to be going perfectly. But then Jim was caught having sex with any female that had a pulse and they could no longer conceal their egregious cash skimming.

Jim got snagged funneling $265,000 in hush money to virginal church secretary Jessica Hahn, in order to cover up their adulterous tryst. Suddenly the Bakkers became pariahs. All of their friends deserted them. Even fellow Assemblies of God minister Jimmy Swaggart (fornicator) took some unnecessary potshots, just for fun and just to be a "pompous ass..."Swaggart went on CNN and told Larry King that Jim was a "cancer in the body of Christ." Of course, as it turned out. Swaggart was much worse than Bakker.

But these two charlatans keep showing up on TV. Both of these "whore-hoppers" are back on TV.

Bakker is back at his old tricks, as "snake oil salesman," peddling everything for trinkets to survival kits, in the Name of the Lord. "He is gifted. You cannot sit in his studio and not see that. His natural ability to connect with the viewer one-on-one is a rare quality. Not everyone in Christian television has that talent." What is so surprising to me is the many "Christians," gullible enough to continue to support this rascal, and not see that he exploits the Christian Faith for his own gains and self-serving interest.

For Bakker, the new show is a far cry from PTL, whose fall revealed the lavish lifestyle he and his ex-wife, Tammy Faye, enjoyed. "I have to die to the flesh," he said. "That's what old Jim Bakker has to do on the air every day. I have had the best of everything, 3,000 employees, the finest talent and equipment. Here I have an audio man who is learning, camera people who have never done this before, the copier is broken, and we don't even have phones yet." Bakker said in the early days of his return.

"With all that, the most awesome thing happens here every day. The presence of the Lord comes into this place and people have been healed, depression lifted, and many come to know the Lord." Bakker added.

Bakker said he believed his return might give people "hope that the past can be the past, that God can use them no matter what they have been through. Lori and I are both broken vessels, but God is using us. He can use anybody -- no matter what."

He said he won't regret trying his hand at television again even if the show doesn't succeed. "If we don't make it, that's fine too," he said. "It would be easy to get a little house in the Ozarks and speak once in a while. But that is not my calling. I have to be true to what God has called me to do, and trust Him with the rest."

In my opinion, Bakker's Claims to fame may be described as a "high-profile televangelist; adulterer; bisexual; fraud; ex-con; ex-Mr. Tammy Faye Bakker.

I can't decide which moral act he violated was worse, the $265,000 hush-money payment to keep church secretary Jessica Hahn quiet about their affair, or the $158 million he embezzled from his own PTL (a.k.a. Praise the Lord, a.k.a. People That Love) ministry? Maybe, it is his hypocrisy and his false Christian doctrine, Bakker will be judged

Jimmy Swaggart

Jimmy Swaggert, pseudo-Christian is a showman, and proven fornicator. He is one of the top so called Christian TV evangelist, who has fallen from grace. He should have followed the careers his cousins, Jerry Lee Lewis, and Mickey Gilley, as no one would have cared about his affairs and he would not be labeled as one of the greatest hypocrites in the ministries After he was caught with the prostitute and he cried on TV he went right back and did it again with another whore. DO NOT send this guy any money no matter how much he cries.

Much of the money, which was meant for his ministry, went to maintain extravagant lifestyles. Swaggart bought himself a $1.5 million mansion. In his show of fatherly affection, he bought another mansion, worth US$700,000 for his son, Donnie with money loaned by his ministry.

CNN aired on Sunday November 2, 1997 a documentary about former Assembly of God Evangelist Jimmy Swaggart whose ministry net worth is one hundred million dollars and is run by the Swaggart family.

Financial statements alone of the Jimmy Swaggart Evangelistic Association do not reveal the fact that Jimmy Swaggart, his wife and his son, earn over six hundred thousand dollars in annual salaries and drive a fleet of six Mercedes Benz. Jimmy Swaggart lied on camera when questioned by CNN about his salary. He stated he was not really drawing a salary although IRS records showed otherwise.

It is a very sad state when prominent TV Evangelists such as Jimmy Swaggart who can shout, dance and preach better than the rest of them lie about their salaries and hide them. In addition the financial statements of JSEA do not reveal that Jimmy Swaggart Ministry loaned Jimmy 4.2 million dollars to build his fancy estate.

Do not be an ignorant foolish emotional Christian and support this character. While I am willing to forgive anyone who has sinned, as I am one of those, I do not and cannot condone any so-called Christian minister using religion for personal gain.

Here is my point: Anytime a church expands its role to include un-Biblical purposes, serving interest of a few, and changes its focus from teaching salvation, to entertaining it congregation, with nonsense humor, fake doctrine; and decides to become a "land-mark monument" by constructing massive buildings, with basketball courts, and recreational centers, and tolerating self-serving, egotistical ministers, it becomes a dangerous and destructive tool for the establishment to exploit for its purposes. It leads people away from God, and enable "ministers," and others so-called religious leaders to prey on women, and children, and/or engage in homosexual relationships, and/or allow the "hidden extortion" of funds to provide an exotic lifestyle for ministerial hierarchy. This is a mockery of Christianity. Like big government or major corporations, "money breed power, power breeds corruption, and corruption breed absolute corruption." Members should keep a diligent watchful eye on the leadership of their church and be mindful of over ambitious minister, who are more interested in a lavish lifestyle and perks than preaching the Gospel.

I apologize to any reader that finds my opinions, and observations offensive, as my intent is to simply expose the truth; not upset anyone. If I have said anything in error, I will further apologize; however, I want evidence that I have misstated facts regarding the content of my assessments and evaluation of "preachers." As a Christian, I simply cannot stand idly by and watch people become victims of schemes by persons using God as a tool to exploit my brothers and sisters in Christ. A special apology to my wife, Kim, as she is a little upset with my exposure of some of those she enjoys reading or watching (Joyce Meyer her favorite, and Meyer is inspirational). However, I must write what I observe – this is my second apology regarding Meyer, and I think my opinion of her is clear.

Lastly, I would be remiss if I did not mentioned Rice Brooks, (Bethel, Morning Star, World Outreach; etc; etc. , Brooks and "gang" – "con artists" and some of the best). His annual salary including wife's income from the Church is reported to be about $600,000, plus unbelievable perks. You want to know more about Rice, ask Ray McCollum (Minister who founded Bethel in Brentwood, Tennessee). I want to thank Mark Holdeman for his help and input in exposing Rice Brooks and his cronies.

Brother Ray, as I refer to him, is, in my opinion, a preacher truly seeking the Lord's will in his life. He has undergone more adversities than most preachers, and has been mistreated by those with whom he placed a great deal of trust. While Ray may not be perfect, and we are not always in agreement, I find him refreshing when comparing other so-called men of God in his teachings and values. Ray is an exception, and is not to be placed in the same category, with Brooks, Hinn, or any of the others mentioned in this chapter.

I REFER TO MOST OF THESE PREACHERS AS "VULTURES OF SATAN, PREYING ON BELIEVERS." Please do not be deceived!! (My opinion)

Why this chapter is necessary: *We the Sheeple* are distracted and misinformed by religion, and religious zealots regarding key political issues, facts, and conclusions. You must remember that these charlatans will do just about anything that serves their best interest, including teaching false doctrines. Some of those I have mentioned will use ignorance of other religions as a tool to justify the actions by political leaders, including declaration of war, and passing pro-Marxist legislation. As a Christian, I suggest that you become skeptical of any religious leader that advocates political violence; or Churches that uses known pro Marxist ministers, as an example to promote peace, and/or social change.

"Howbeit when he, the Spirit of truth, is dome, he will guide you into all truth: for he shall not speak of himself; but whatsoever he shall hear, that shall he speak: and he will shew you things to come" (Jn. 16: 13).

You can find out more about how Christians are exploited, by reading my notes, which I will send to you free. My research notes will expose phonies, such as Joel Osteen, Billy Graham, Franklin Graham, and others – all Charlatans, in my opinion...

I take no pleasure in exposing these so called Christian leaders. I find it a shame and I am disappointed that too many good people are falling for the miscued teachings of "charlatans." Many, if not most of the so called men of God are "wolves in sheep's clothing."

The reason that I have included these "scam artist" in my book is that most are used by the establishment to make sheeple out of us all and create a mentality of just accepting what we hear, without questioning motives. They are used to create fear of Muslims, and "other enemies" created by the establishment. On the "flip side" these same globalist manipulate Muslims, atheist, and others to view Christians as an enemy, and through fear, they divide and conquer, for control of global resources. I think I make it obvious that I am not pro-Muslim, and do not misunderstand what I have stated, but I want you to understand how religion is used to justify wars, and promote political agendas of the "Elitist."

CHAPTER FIVE:
WHY WAR?

"War against a foreign country only happens when the moneyed classes think they are going to profit from it." George Orwell

I have often pondered the question, "Why do we have wars?" I have heard many theories about the reasons for war, but it is still a mystery to me. Theories stated by more than just historians; theories from anthropologist, sociologist, archeologist, theologians, and economist. One of my friends, Doug Stutson, a retired professor of economics, believes that wars are fought for strictly for economic reasons, which I believe has some creditability, but only to an extent. I am not sure that a person would be willing to sacrifice the life of his family, or give up his own life, strictly for economic gains. I do think that "those leaders" who the "Sheeple" follow do engage in war for economic gains, but only for "those in power." We know that the average person gains little from war, even when on the winning side. Innately, man may be a born predator, with an inherent desire to "hunt and kill;" possess territory, and have "his choice of a mate," as some sociologist and anthropologist believe, and "war" is just in his "nature;" but I do not think that man would organize or ban together just for the sake of killing without being motivated. Nor do I think that wars are fought for just religious reasons, as some of the theologians believe. I do believe, however, that religion is uses as a tool to justify wars and killing, but is not the motivating factor behind a war. People must be motivated to engage in war; by fear, by greed, by threat of losing "territory," and many times by religion.

The inherent fallacy in the equality of men is their tendency to fall into the two groups, i.e., "leaders and followers." The latter constitute the vast majority, and, by far, followers outnumber leaders. The followers (the "sheeple") stand in need of authority which will make decisions for them, as the majorities are subjects to feelings of inferior, and ineptness. Most followers are insecure, honest, and have a conscious; while leaders are fearless, and most have sociopathic tendencies. Leaders may also possess a strong "death wish." "The Sheeple" will follow anyone demonstrating leadership qualities, is forceful, and articulate enough motivating reasons for war to convince the majority to follow his/her directions. But, how can anyone be convinced that it is in his best interest to organize for the sole purpose of killing other human beings, and how are they motivated to die for a cause? What tool are methods are used to cause one country to rise up against another? Let's explore the answer.

"In 1931 the Permanent Committee on Literature and the Arts of the League of Nations proposed exchanges of letters between intellectuals. Contacted in June 1932, Freud agreed to respond to letter from Albert Einstein, which he received in August. The result was a "Letter to Albert Einstein" titled "Why War?" On September 8, 1932, Freud stated to Max Eitingon that he had finally finished writing the "tedious and sterile so-called discussion with Einstein" (quoted in Jones, 1957, Vol. 3, p. 185). To Einstein's question "Is there any way of delivering mankind from the menace of war?" (1933b [1932], p. 199), Freud responded by returning to a number of issues that he had already addressed in his work on this subject, from "Thoughts for the Times on War and Death" (1915b) to *Civilization and Its Discontents* (1930a). Rather than his correspondent's proposal to consider the relationship between "right and might," he preferred to consider the relationship between right and violence ("Might replaces Right"), and he argued that as distinct from the primitive law of the strongest, "right is the might of a community" (p. 205). But right itself cannot be exercised without violence. The wish to prevent war was no doubt embodied in the League of Nations, but that organization remained impotent, except on the level of ideas." (Source: Internet – with slight changes)

It is my belief that the reason for WWI, instigated by the "Power Elite" was to create global conditions so horrific that the world's population would welcome a world government to maintain permanent peace, using principles of Progressives. Since Marxism was not accepted by most of the population in the United States, WWII was necessary. Please note that the United States has not declared a war since WWII, Korea, Viet Nam, Afghanistan and Iraq are considered "police actions." We do have "A war on Terror," whatever that means – "propaganda to maintain fear of an attack from radical Muslims in order to pass legislation depriving us of our Constitutional rights, and to diminish freedoms." A threat of war creates a need for government protection, regardless of the cost.

According to Freud, Einstein was correct in positing an instinct of hate in humankind, a notion that fit with "our mythological theory of the instincts" (p. 212). "The death instinct turns into the destructive instinct when, with the help of special organs, it is directed outwards on to objects; the organism preserves its own life, so to say, by destroying an extraneous one" (p. 211). This was a factual circumstance that had to be taken into account; the Bolshevist utopia clearly pointed up the illusion of egalitarian material satisfaction.

Freud acknowledged that he did not have much to propose: "We are pacifists because we are obliged to be for organic reasons" (p. 214). "We are shaped by the long process of the development of civilization, to which we owe the best of what we have become, as well as a good part of what we suffer from." (From the Internet).

Pacifists have a great deal in common when it comes to politics. Unfortunately, pacifist are used for the purpose of an agenda, which is usually one espoused by Communist. Members of "The Establishment" advocates that "more care should be taken to educate an upper stratum of men with independent minds, not open to intimidation and eager in the pursuit of truth, whose business it would be to give direction to the dependent masses. It goes without saying that the encroachments made by the executive power of the State and the prohibition laid by the Church upon freedom of thought are far from propitious for the production of a class of this kind. The ideal condition of things would of course be a community of men who had subordinated their instinctual life to the dictatorship of reason." – Freud. Notice how the principles of Marx are subconsciously planted into the thinking of intellectual pacifist. Freud continues, "Nothing else could unite men so completely and so tenaciously, even if there were no emotional ties between them. But in all probability that is a Utopian expectation" (1933b, p. 212-213)."

In London in 1948 it was suggested that political leaders be systematically required to undergo psychoanalysis. This naturally elicited particularly acute reactions among psychiatrists who were members of the French Communist Party.. (Source: Internet)

Read this again, "According to Freud, Einstein was correct in positing an instinct of hate in humankind, a notion that fit with "our mythological theory of the instincts" (p. 212). "The death instinct turns into the destructive instinct when, with the help of special organs, it is directed outwards on to objects. The organism preserves its own life, so to say, by destroying an extraneous one" (p. 211), this was a factual circumstance that had to be taken into account; the Bolshevist utopia clearly pointed up the illusion of egalitarian material satisfaction." ---

Source Citation: Freud, Sigmund. (1933b [1932]). "Warum Kreig? (Brief an Albert Einstein [sept. 1932]), Warum Kreig? Pourquoi la guerre? Why War? Paris: Internationales Institute für gestige Zusammenarbeit am Völkerbund (Institute for International Cooperation); GW, 16: 13-27; Why war? SE,22:197-215.

Bibliography Freud, Sigmund. (1915b). Thoughts for the times on war and death. SE, 14: 273-300.———. (1930a [1929]). *Civilization and its discontents*. SE, 21: 57-145. Freud, Sigmund, and Bullitt, William. (1966b [1938]). Introduction. In their Thomas Woodrow Wilson, twenty-eighth president of the United States: A psychological study (pp. xi xvi). New York: Weidenfeld and Nicholson. Jones, Ernest. (1957). Sigmund Freud: Life and work. London: Hogarth. —ALAINDE MIJOLLA

Without being too redundant, let me partially repeat what has already been stated. "It is obvious to me, that WWI was necessary to cause such destruction that no one would ever want a world war again. It has been stated that WWI was the war to end all wars. Based on the forgoing, it was well planned by the PE to establish a foundation for The New World Order, the League of Nations, but it failed making WWII necessary; thus the UN was founded."

"When a war ends, friends become enemies, and enemies become friends".

The Iron Mountain Report, which makes more sense to me as to why we have wars than most of what I have researched, discusses the necessity of a "war system" for the management of society, and controlling the population. It ponders the elite's question of what alternatives can be implemented to manage human populations should peace prevail over the maintenance of the "war system?" As the foreword explains, "War fills certain functions essential to the stability of our society; until other ways of filling them are developed; the "war system" must be maintained -- and improved in effectiveness." Since WWII no war the US has engaged was declared and is unconstitutional, as stated earlier. Thus far, the United States has managed to lose in every police action in which we have participated; however, I feel this is by intent to destroy the people's will to fight, and to convince the people the need for a strong government to protect their freedoms, and eventually find the only solution to security is a "World Government;" meanwhile, in reality, these "wars," including the "War on Terror (like the "War on Poverty") is used in passing legislation to destroy freedoms, and to make us "Sheeple."

Therefore, Peace is a threat to the globalist's agenda. Peace exists when there is a lack of ambition -- individually, or as a society -- to violate others for profit, power, resources or territory. It is something the globalist managers are not yet prepared to deal with. Their history is one of personal and societal violations. In Quigley's book, "Tragedy and Hope," the position of the insiders is explained. It is the tragedy of war that brings the hope of peace, which can only be accomplished by allowing the "insiders" to control the world's natural resources, the currency, set the policies of all governments; and controls the population. Why else would there be a push for a national health plan managed by bureaucrats, if not to control population growth. In fact, the final plan, before declaring a "Unitarian Government" may be to ignite a nuclear war, as this may be the only solution to bring the world's population to a number acceptable to the "Elitist;" one humbled and easy to control.

The full report from Iron Mountain provides greater detail of the elite's plans and motives, but the following gives a glimpse of mentality of the "Globalist": "War is not, as is widely assumed, primarily an instrument of policy utilized by nations to extend or defend their expressed political values or their economic interests. On the contrary, it is itself the principle basis of organization on which all modern societies is constructed...At the root of all ostensible differences of national interest lie the dynamic requirements of the "war system" itself for periodic armed conflict. Readiness for war characterizes contemporary social systems more broadly than their economic and political structures...Economic analyses of the anticipated problems of transition to peace have not recognized the broad pre-eminence of war in the definition of social systems. The PE has determined the best system to accomplish its goals is to institute the principles of Marx and Engels, as these principles are most appealing to the majority of the politically ignorant people (most of the world's population). The people are fooled into thinking that government can and will provide all of their needs. The...real situation of conversion to...peace...can be developed only from the premise of full understanding of the nature of the "war system" it proposes to abolish, which in turn presupposes detailed comprehension of the functions the "war system" performs for society. It will require the construction of a detailed and feasible system of substitutes for those functions that are necessary to the stability and survival of human societies..." This is where the government promises a utopia, and the use of Marx's ideology replaces war.

When this report was first published our nation and its adversaries were well defined. There was a "cold war" to bind us together with "us" against "them" worldview. In this age of "Globalism," trade treaties, the WTO, the G-8, the IMF, the World Bank and the UN have begun to supersede national sovereignty, making our own rule of law (the Constitution) obsolete and subordinated to a Universal Law established by the "Power Elite."

"War has provided both ancient and modern societies with a dependable system for stabilizing and controlling national economies, the people. No alternate method of control has yet been tested in a complex modern economy that has shown itself remotely comparable in scope, or effectiveness. War or the threat of war and the permanent possibility of war is the foundation for stable government; it supplies the basis for general acceptance of political authority. It has enabled societies to maintain necessary class distinctions, and it has ensured the subordination of the citizen to the state... No modern political ruling group has successfully controlled its constituency after failing to sustain the continuing credibility of an external threat of war... As the most formidable of threats to life itself...the war system has provided the machinery through which the motivational forces governing human behavior have been translated into binding social allegiance. War or the continuing threat of war gives the establishment complete control over the "masses."

Prior to September 11, 2001, our people were losing their faith in the American government. The seemingly different faces of Democrats and Republicans became blurred by the corruption, deceit and broken promises of both sides and at all levels of government. People were tired of being manipulated by bureaucrats and judges, who misinterpreted the laws to suit a political agenda. Our faith in the fiat economy was on the verge of a collapse. With the trauma based conditioning of the WTC attack and a new "terrorist" enemy to unite us, the disintegration of our hollow economy and political institutions has been postponed. There was an uplifting and now, we are faced with a total collapse, and further loss of freedoms, as a result of legislation passed after 9/11/ . If you can't understand what is happening, you are totally politically stupid.

"Discussion of the ways and means of transitions to such a [warless] world is meaningless unless, a) substitute institutions can be devised to fill these functions, or b) it can reasonably be hypothecated that the loss or partial loss of any one function need not destroy the viability of future societies..." Is this not happening before our very eyes today? "An acceptable economic surrogate for the war system will require the expenditure of resources for completely nonproductive purposes at a level comparable to that of the military expenditures otherwise demanded by the size and complexity of each society. Such a substitute system of apparent "waste" must be of a nature that will permit it to remain independent of the normal supply-demand economy; it must be subject to arbitrary political control." Pay attention to our debt, deficits, uncontrolled spending on useless projects, and total corruption in government. We are almost in the hand of "International dictators."

Thus, an introduction to Marxism or a system which promised a security for all, along with a utopian society is the blue-print used by the Elitist to capture the conscious of freemen. Of course, once accepted by the masses, it is not easy to recapture individual freedoms sacrificed for a promise of security and peace. We need a political revolution!

The fact is, advances in technology may prevent an all out war, until "the establishment's elitist" decides it is not feasible to have peace because the world is over-populated and a nuclear war is needed to reduce the world's population to a manageable size. In the age of mutually assured destruction, the major war powers must limit their activities to "police actions," until a controllable nuclear war can be propelled to only kill those undesirables Kissinger spoke of in his dissertation regarding population reduction. Again, let me repeat, "Do you realize that congress has not declared a war since WWII, but we have been in numerous wars?" We no longer have genuine national "defense," a UN "peacekeeping" missions been substituted to "waste" our excess industrial/military capacity under arbitrary political control, but these surrogate mini-wars have irritated most of the American people. They are no longer an effective substitute system for war. It is necessary for the Power Elitist to keep the threat of terrorism, war, or complete destruction of our nation in the minds of the people to keep them under control. A substitute for war may be unlimited social programs, such as healthcare, welfare, education, and redistribution of wealth, but this will not be enough to generate supply and demand of goods and services. So, what is the answer? It may well be a planned reduction of the world's population, suddenly set off by an attack on Israel or an attack by Israel on Iran.

"A viable political substitute for war must posit a generalized external menace to each society of a nature and degree sufficient to require the organization and acceptance of political authority... [A] Credible substitute for war must generate an omnipresent and readily understood fear of personal destruction," as mentioned above.... "A substitute for war in its function as the uniquely human system of population control must ensure the survival, if not the improvement, of the species, in terms of its relation to environmental supply... The only apparent problem in the application of an adequate eugenic substitute for war is that of timing; it cannot be effectuated until the transition to peace has been completed, which involves a serious temporary risk of ecological failure..." You must read all you can about population control as advocated by David Rockefeller, Henry Kissinger and other "insiders." With a controlled population, there would be controlled supply and a controlled demand for goods and services, which would be easier to manage. With an "International Health Plan," the PE could determine who lives and who dies, racial demographics, and the number of births needed to sustain a desired world's population.

Have we transitioned to a state of peace through contentedly consuming the bounty of the global marketers? Well, it does appear that the superpower nations are settling for economic competition for global markets, rather than provoking acts of war against other superpowers, but, then why continue the buildup of the military in these countries? What adequate eugenic substitute do the "Global Managers" have in store for us? Are they preparing us for the next wave, with news stories about the threat of "terrorist" activated bio-warfare? Has this terrorist menace been sufficient to restore the acceptance of our political authorities? Are not Americans falling hook, line and sinker for all the media delivered, political diatribe that is striking a major blow to the Bill of Rights? Just look at the legislation passed after 9/11 and you have the answer, but wait, is this enough to control the population growth of the world? Not hardly; especially, when you consider the fact that the PE feels that a global population of about six hundred million is sufficient. This would require the elimination of about 90% of the world's population. On October 2nd **1979**, Robert McNamara (President of the World Bank) addressed a group of international bankers thus: "We can begin with the most critical problem of all, population growth" ..Concluding that ".either the current birth rates must come down more quickly, or the death rates must go up...There are, of course, many ways in which the death rates can go up. In a thermonuclear age, we can accomplish it very quickly and decisively" (as indeed has been done in Hiroshima and Nagasaki in1945). Is this the next step for "The New World Order?"

"[The war system cannot responsibly be allowed to disappear] until, 1) we know exactly what it is we plan to put in its place, and 2) we are certain, beyond reasonable doubt, that these substitute institutions will serve their purposes in terms of the survival and stability of society... Some observers, in fact, believe that it cannot be... [Allowed to disappear] at all in our time; that the price of peace is, simply, too high... It is uncertain, at this time, whether peace will ever be possible;" unless, of course, the population can be reduced to a manageable size, and divided and controlled into groups to serve the Power Elitist, after all, whoever is left in the world must have food, water, housing, and the luxuries of life provided for the PE; "[However], it is possible that one or more major sovereign nations may arrive, through ambiguous leadership, at a position in which a ruling administrative class may lose control of basic public opinion or of its ability to rationalize a desired war... As the report from Iron Mountain made clear, this could be catastrophic."

To whom would peace be catastrophic? How high is the price of peace? It would seem to cost the citizens nothing, but the "ruling administrative class" could lose everything they have "worked" so hard for. Perhaps in recognition of that, the "Elite" are not yet prepared for peace and need more time for such a transition. The talking heads are already calling this war on terrorism the "Hundred Years War." Unless, the population is reduced to a manageable size, just as Ayn Rand described in her book, "Anthem," or we can get rid of the PE, peace is not feasible, and, is not desirable, if the only way to peace is under the conditions described by Ayn Rand.

"It seems evident that, in the event an important part of the world is suddenly plunged without sufficient warning into an inadvertent peace, even partial and inadequate preparation for the possibility may be better than none." However, the plan rest in the hands of those who control the currencies and major political systems of the world.

There are still too many unanswered question, in my opinion, to tell who is ultimately answerable for the events of September 11. Was the ruling administrative class behind the event or have they merely taken full advantage of the situation? Just to ask the question, will bring "the powers to be" down on you with a force to make you ashamed that you even asked the question. The questions will probably remain unanswered for some time, like the JFK assassination, Waco and the OK City bombing (just never refer to any of these act as a conspiracy, if you do you will be labeled a radical nutcase). You must accept the facts, determined by a controlled media and "the establishment," that all of history happens by accident and assassinations occur because of a lone crazed gunman. But, as the wave of the New World Order crests in its final assault upon its newfound dominion, there is on the horizon a war; a war like no other; an "Iron Mountain" war.

Wars are the norm. Peace is a short period of time between wars. The need for war is always created by those elitist psychopaths who are motivated by greed and power. The charge to battle is not led by the politician, or bureaucrats who create them, but by our young men and women, misled into thinking they are giving their lives for freedoms. Iraq is a good example. Iraq was never a threat to the United States, and those "propagandist," who claim that the world is better off with

Saddam Hussein dead, should remember that we lost none of our young men and women when he controlled Iraq, and the country was safe (I know as I was there twice after the first Persian Gulf War). Saddam was a secular Muslim and wanted only to keep Iraq sovereign, and free from occupation. He was an ally, which our government betrayed. We should have worked out the Israel-Iraq problems and kept him in power - had we done this no American lives would have been lost in Iraq… There were no WMD! Enemies are created to place fear in the hearts of the people to keep them thinking the government is their great protector. War is a great tool of the Power Elite.

"We must annex those people. We can afflict them with our wise and beneficent government. We can introduce the novelty of thieves, all the way up from street-car pickpockets to municipal robbers and Government defaulters, and show them how amusing it is to arrest them and try them and then turn them loose -- some for cash and some for political influence. We can make them ashamed of their simple and primitive justice. We can make that little bunch of sleepy islands the hottest corner on earth, and array it in the moral splendor of our high and holy civilization. Annexation is what the poor islanders need. Shall we to men benighted, the lamp of life deny?" - __Mark Twain__

(Some of the foregoing was taken from the Internet) If you want greater details, regarding why wars are fought, please request my research papers and notes used to write this book, they are free – email your request to braunkenh@aol.com.

CHAPTER SIX:
FROM A REPUBIC TO WHAT?

"It is in vain, sir, to extenuate the matter. Gentlemen may cry, "Peace! Peace!" – But there is no peace. The war is actually begun! The next gale that sweeps from the north will bring to our ears the clash of resounding arms! Our brethren are already in the field! Why stand we here idle? What is it that gentlemen wish? What would they have? Is life so dear, or peace so sweet, as to be purchased at the price of chains and slavery? Forbid it, Almighty God! I know not what course others may take; but as for me, give me liberty, or give me death!" These words were spoken by Patrick Henry, on March 23, 1775 in his cry to unite the Colonies against tyranny. The King of England had imposed unfair taxation on the people and set out to deprive the colonist of God given freedoms, i.e., the right to life, liberty, and pursuit of happiness. Their cry rang thorough out the land, "no taxation without representation." They knew well that regulations, and taxation brings oppression.

Liberty has underpinned the "Christian" ideal for millennia, and it was the idea of liberty that established Europe, including England. Countries were forged by people's desire for freedoms, and the British leadership in politics flowed out of the Revolution of 1688 (often referred to as the 'Glorious Revolution of 1688'), which established a "Bill of Rights" and the rule of law (An Act Declaring the Rights and Liberties of the Subject and Settling the Succession of the Crown). Let us not forget that our liberty, and our freedoms are constantly under threat from governments and their apologists who seek to control the populations by over-taxing, over-regulating, by force, and/or by whatever means necessary, this will never changes... It will always be, "those who want to control against those who want to be free!"

From the very beginning of civilization and recording of history, there has been "a war," a war between "freedom and tyranny!" Currently, in the United States and throughout the world, there is a struggle between those who want to "rule" against those who desire to live free. After centuries of revolutions and uprisings, people are not yet free from the fear of loss of liberties. Anxiety, hangs like a cloud over us because of continued pressures from economic and political policies instituted by non-producing bureaucrats, and lawmakers who, like parasites, feed on the efforts of productivity and responsible people. When "privileged people" are empowered with control of the economic and political system of a nation, freedoms and liberties diminish quickly. It has always been the same, in every political system. All governments (kings, dictators, elected officials, etc., etc.) still threaten the populace with stiff fines, penalties, or prison unless the people comply with self-serving laws, and taxations that most of the people feel unfair, do not want, and/or feel these many laws are unnecessary, and destructive to individual freedoms; laws that enables the creation of a "legal" fiat monetary system, corrupting our economic systems, and robs individuals of their savings, via a Pro-Marxist income tax. These laws and regulations are passed and instituted by a political system to control, restrict, and usurps freedoms from the people. We are forced to pay taxes on what we earn, and pay a tax on property that we own, under the threat of not doing so; we will be imprisoned, or, in the case of property tax, will lose our property. Why is it fair for the government to charge me "rent" on property, for which I have already paid, and if I fail to pay "my rent, i.e., property tax," the government will take my property from me, and auction it off on the court house steps? How is this fair? It is not fair, and is not what our "Founders" intended. What is even worse is that the government will take from our earnings, and "put a portion of it in the pockets of those who do nothing but create tax burdens," and spend the rest on programs most do not want or need. We are required by "law" to buy documents to travel (a passport) to other countries; to pay for a license to drive a car; and to fill out government tax forms to get a job (W-4). There are other, many more, schemes the government enforces to "take what we earn" to satisfy its greed; "license fees and permit requirements, which we must purchase from the government to conduct business, or to buy and sell; taxes on utilities; telephone use; and most items purchased."

Meanwhile the spending by government is never reduced; it only increases, as the tax burden on citizens grows. It is so ironic to hear the politicians and "power-hungry" bureaucrats tout the claims of how free and great the United States is, but, yet, we find ourselves "enslaved" in insurmountable debt, high unemployment, and many "underemployed." We find ourselves in useless and winless wars, protecting the borders of other countries, while not concerned with protecting our own. There are so many government agencies, programs, and non-productive jobs in the government, that it takes more money than the government can generate to support this great bureaucracy of greed and corruption; they, the "political establishment," are spending more money than the government can "print or tax," and continues "increasing the supply of a fiat currency" at an unthinkable rate, which diminishes the purchasing power of the money people earn and save. The government's monetary policies have destroyed the savings and wealth of the middle class. We watch our savings being reduced by 10% or better per year in buying power (do not believe the governments numbers on the inflation rate, as they are manipulated), and the debt is increasing at a rapid rate. It is estimated that our debt will soar to $24 Trillion Dollars in less than ten years (2020). I believe that we have already reached this number (2010) and the global debt is 17 times greater than the world's GDP. There is no way out, if we continue with the same policies currently in place, with the same agencies, and political cronies in charge. I believe the debt, included unfunded programs, and obligations exceed $60 trillion. We may not be able to recover, and remain free.

Glenn Beck has it completely wrong when he insists that a flat tax on income is better than a consumption tax. A tax on earnings places the government in control of our income, It, the government, has first call on every dime we make, and if we fail to pay, we go to jail or have our assets confiscated. The same is true with property. Why give the government control of your property? Our founders would call this treason and tyranny at its best. No, we should have control of our earnings, our property, or our assets, and the government should have no power to take any of these from us, for any reason. Beck claims to be Constitutionalist and an anti-Marxist, but how can he be when he advocates that the government have control of the earnings of individuals. George Bernard Shaw and the Fabian Society would use the Becks of the world, and their naïve understanding of tax system to give the perception that a tax on income is a conservative and constitutional accepted policy- it is not! The principle is Marxist!!

If continued, the current rate of spending and expansion by the government will eventually collapse our economic system. It is my belief, however, that this collapse is the deliberate goal of those who control our political and economic system. I believe that the "insiders" fully understand that in order to convince the average patriotic American to accept the United States' position in "The New World Order," these "power parasites" must make conditions so horrible that the people will agree to any solution to restore "security and peace," even openly accepting the principles of Marxism, which are already fomented in our political and economical system, but somewhat hidden, and disguised.. The "Insiders" have one goal and that is dominion over the world's natural resources; a one world government, which "they" control. Glenn Beck refers to the "insiders," as "Progressives." It matters not what name they are given, the agenda is the same. Only a duck walks like a duck, quacks like a duck, looks like a duck; and by any other name is still a duck. Same is true of the "Globalist Insiders."

I have disclose, and will continue tell the story of how we are becoming (have become) a Marxist globalist society, with strong supporting evidence, and how "Progressive" policies effect all of us, but more importantly, how it effects future generations. Our heirs will be enslaved by a corrupt evil empire. We are in the "fourth quarter." We must act now!!

You may think, "It will never happen here; our freedoms will not be lost." It is happening now, as I write these words. Had you lived in the 1940's, and 50's, you would have never thought that we would have "forced integration," or a decay of moral values; morals so eroded that we have laws which allow same sex marriage; and I never dreamed that I would live in a time that the killing of unborn babies, for the sake of convenience, by abortion, is legal. Sixty years ago, no one would have believed that we would be trading with "our enemies," providing them with financial aid, promoting their economy to the extent that they become stronger than we, but we have, and we are rapidly moving in a direction of a "third world" economy.

Rand Paul has it wrong, also. When asked if he would have supported the Civil Rights Act, had he been in Congress at the time, he replied, "Yes;" as a true Constitutionalist, he should have said, "No," as the Act is unconstitutional.

I want to be clear, "I believe in equal protection under the law for all; but special privileges for none." No one should deprive any deserving person equal rights under the law; however, no one should be given special consideration, or granted special privileges, for any reason.

Moral decay, distractions from truth and progressive parasites in America are responsible for depleting our rights under the Constitution, and leading us down this path to "political enslavement." The movement has evolved slowly, and deliberately. We are distracted from the truth by entertainment and deceitful news commentators because we have become complacent, and morally lazy, due to a rather secured life and have enjoyed an extended time of prosperity, allowing us too much leisure. We have become sluggish in seeking the truth that keeps men free. In fact, the Constitution has become that "pesky" piece of paper that political appointees to the Supreme Court "misinterprets" and ruled so many times against its intent that it is almost obsolete. An example of how morals have diminished is remembering back when profanity was not allowed spoken in public places; and "taking God's name in vain" was considered a sin. Today, many not only think that "using God's name in vain is not a sin," but actually use His name in vain openly and freely as part of their vocabulary; this is especially true in the entertainment business. Progressives, and degenerates are able to show obscenities in the theaters, on TV, and use vulgar and profane language because of the Courts "misinterpretation" of the First Amendment; hiding behind "free speech." Please understand why we have "free speech." Freedom of speech is a "Constitutional Right" because our Founders did not want to limit, or restrict individual from speaking out against the government; "freedom of speech" did not become an amendment to our Constitution to allow "smut peddlers" the right to promote immorality, obscenities, and profanity. My, how this "right" changed!

Loss of freedoms begins with "taxation," and carries all the way through "to how the elections" of "professional politicians are controlled" by a well established "political machine," which is interested only in maintaining its power, and "extorting" our earnings, by politicians taxing us ever how much these "greedy maggot" decide. These "parasites" do nothing more than tax and spend; and spend and tax at every opportunity. They establish agencies and bureaucracies that have one purpose and that is to generate money through, useless programs, winless wars, license fees, filing fees, taxation, and creating more fiat money (called "dollars"); passing laws, and manipulating the voting system in order to control the people. They produce nothing and take everything they can. They are "worthless non-producers," but dangerous, as they are all members of the same network, which "sucks up all it can;" but, unfortunately, are in control of our nation! We let it happen!!

Remember, it is taxation that is the life blood of these "blood sucking" politicians, and the parasitic bureaucrats; taxes, along with printing fiat currency (money with no store of value). The more the bureaucrats are able to tax, the more control they have over individual lives. Patrick Henry understood this when he made his famous speech in 1775, and I hope you understand the danger of unlimited power to tax today. Without the government having that power, which we have foolish given it, to take a part of what we earn, it cannot have the power to deprive us of freedoms, and "steal" our earnings, and property. In the following pages, I have explained how we the people have allowed the "global financial parasites," these "progressives," to steal the wealth of the average working American by deceit; and use us to expand their agenda, which will lead us into "The New World Order," a one world government, making each of us "serfs" to their economic and political system controlled by "Elitist."

Many of the colonists wanted nothing but peace and were willing to give up their freedoms in exchange for security and the promise of peace; just as many of us are willing to do today. Fortunately, there were a few brave men who stood up to the oppressive British Parliament and became the Founding Fathers of our Republic (which did not last long), These brave men were willing to die for a cause, which they believe in, and set aside their own agenda to become part of a revolution that established a nation, which supposedly would serve the best interest of the people, and provide alienable rights to all citizens. These God given rights are the right to life, liberty, and the pursuit of happiness – "that's it," no "government health-care plan, no Medicare, no Social Security, and no guarantee of a job." Nothing Marxist!!! Do we have any brave ment today to stand against this tyrannical government of ghoulish politicians, and bureaucrats?

Patrick Henry served as a delegate to the Continental Congress (1774-76) and the Virginia provincial convention (1775). He served two terms, as governor of Virginia (1776-79 and 1784-86). Patrick Henry understood the danger in a strong central government. In fact, originally, Henry opposed ratification of the U.S. Constitution, believing that it endangered the sovereignty of the States; so, he worked successfully to add the first 10 amendments, known as the Bill of Rights, to the Constitution, with the hope of preserving States Rights and individual freedoms. He was a great American, and we need a present day Patrick Henry as we are no longer a Republic represented by elected official who serve the best interest of all the people. Elections are controlled by strong political machines in every state. If a person running for office is not a member of the "good old boy network," it is almost impossible for him/her to get elected. James Madison was right in the mix of protecting individual freedoms. You must read "The Federalist Papers." Who will stand up and lead a revolt against today's political machine, controlled by one party with two names (Republican and Democrats alike)?

Before the first shots were fired of what would become the war for independence in April 1775, patriots had been gathering arms to fight the British if that became necessary. General Thomas Gage, commander of British forces in Boston, had been cautious about provoking Colonist. For some months before that clash at Lexington and Concord, patriots were training to fight the British. General Thomas Gage, commander of British forces around Boston, had been careful not to stir-up the Colonist. In April, however, Gage received orders to arrest several patriot leaders. Gage sent his troops out on the night of April 18, hoping to catch the colonists by surprise and thus avoid bloodshed. When the British arrived in Lexington, however, colonial militia awaited them. A battle broke out, but even then, it was not obvious that this clash would lead to war. Many Colonists did not want to declare their independence, as they were afraid of losing, or just felt loyalty to the British. Many wanted to declare independence immediately; others hoped for a quick reconciliation. Like today's voters, there were mixed emotions, even when freedoms were threatened, just as they are now. There are many who do not want to believe or accept the fact that our freedoms are diminishing at a rapid pace. We need patriots to rally to the cause, just as the early colonist rallied to defeat the British at Lexington and Concord --- we need to rally to defeat the enemy in Washington, D.C.

So, "The War of Independence" officially began in 1775, but the signing of the Declaration of Independence on the 4th July 1776 is still celebrated today as a milestone in America's quest for liberty and Independence. The war ended when Cornwallis's surrender at Yorktown in 1781, which formally drew to a close in 1783 when the Treaty of Paris was signed. Every

Fourth of July, we celebrate our nation's independence; however, not many Americans understand, or have read much about the history of our once great nation, and because of ignorance and apathy, we may soon become nothing more than a third world nation, unless we "Wake-up Now." What we learn from history is that we do not learn from history and repeat the same mistakes that civilizations have made before us (We rise from bondage, only to return to bondage). I pray this will change! We need a resigning of our Declaration of Independence, and make the politicians surrender our rights back over to us – the right to own property and the right to keep what we earn.

"The Treaty of Paris, signed on September 3, 1783, ratified by the Congress of the Confederation on 14 January 1784 and by the King of Great Britain on 9, April 1784 (the ratification documents were exchanged in Paris on 12, May 1784), formally ended the American Revolutionary War between the Kingdom of Great Britain and the United States of America, which had rebelled against British rule. The other combatant nations, France, Spain and the Dutch Republic had separate agreements; for details of these, and the negotiations which produced all four treaties view the source of this information." (From Wikipedia, the free encyclopedia). Thus, our nation was born, but where are we now? We now are a part of an "Oligarchy Empire!" Please read, one more time, "The Ten Planks of Communism."

In *The Federalist* (<u>no. 55</u>) which merits quoting here--as follows:

"As there is a degree of depravity in mankind which requires a certain degree of circumspection and distrust: So there are other qualities in human nature, which justify a certain portion of esteem and confidence; Republican government (that of a Republic) presupposes the existence of these qualities in a higher degree than any other form. Were the pictures which have been drawn by the political jealousy of some among us, faithful likenesses of the human character, the inference would be that there is not sufficient virtue among men for self government; and that nothing less than the chains of despotism can restrain them from destroying and devouring one another." (Emphasis added.)

CHAPTER SEVEN:
THE REAL ENEMY

(a special thanks to Bruce Kolinski for allowing me to use a great deal of information sent to me by email – with his permission of course)

Can you guess who the real enemies are? The Muslims, terrorist, or maybe, Iran, you say! Well, you are wrong. The enemy is not in the Middle East, the enemy are the International-financial coterie, and their puppets, in Washington, D.C., and I will name few, starting with White House, Congress, and the Supreme Court. Not too far behind we have the IRS, SEC, Department of Defense, The State Department, CIA, FBI, Department of Energy, Department of Agriculture, The Treasury Department, and the Federal Reserve System. Of course, I left out many others, which should be included... My favorite international maggot is David Rockefeller. Here is a quote from David, *"For more than a century, ideological extremists at either end of the political spectrum have seized upon well-publicized incidents to attack the Rockefeller family for the inordinate influence they claim we wield over American political and economic institutions. Some even believe we are part of a secret cabal working against the best interests of the United States, characterizing my family and me as 'internationalists' and of conspiring with others around the world to build a more integrated global political and economic structure - one world, if you will. If that's the charge, I stand guilty, and I am proud of it." David Rockefeller, Memoirs, 2002.*

Have a look at some of our enemies in D.C. (such as Bush –both of them-, many of the others, including the international parasites, are named throughout this book):

Obama

According to the polls, 56% of the nation agrees that Obama's policies are dismally failed policies (as of 8/20/2010). Personally, I find it frightening that 44% of Americans, statistically at least, still think this America hating Marxist, with legs nesting in the People's White House, and his traitorous Congress, are performing well.. It concerns me that so many in our "rapidly sinking boat," the United Soviet States of Obama, cannot see that Barack Hussein Obama is not incompetent at all, but that he is personally devoid of conscience, completely lacking in integrity, devious, manipulative, arrogant, follows Marxist principles, and destructively hateful. He is dangerous and poses an imminent threat to our nation's freedoms; more so than George Bush, which is hard to believe. He is a heavily indoctrinated Communist organizer trained almost from birth not to care about anything, but his agenda, and to lie, deceive and destroy at any cost to achieve his purpose.

If the "national "de"press corp." had done its job and vetted Obama "We the Sheeple" would have quickly learned that this man, Barry Soetoro, aka, Barry Obama, aka, Barack Hussein Obama is an unfortunate soul, so irreparably and pitifully damaged by his childhood experience at the hands of ideologically warped, Marxist/Muslim parents and their friends, that there can be little hope that he could ever be functional in any healthy, constructive way.

His acts of deliberately violating the Constitution is an act of treason, but no congressman has the courage to stand up to him and press charges, as they all fear the political appointees on the un-Supreme Court (political controlled Federal Courts) would not uphold a conviction against this degenerate half Negro, half Caucasian Marxist. It is not politically correct and one would be charge with a hate crime or be called a racist for bringing forth the charge. Nevertheless, he is a traitor and committed perjury when he took the oath to uphold the Constitution.

If there had been any truth in the Media, we would have learned that this emotionally impoverished narcissist had been surrounded by, and was taken advantage of, by heartless, brainwashed leftists who have no idea how to create anything or build anything; but only study, learn and live to transform America to a Marxist society. They want to destroy our Constitution, criticize and destroy the very principles of freedoms provided by our Founders; they act like evil little energizer bunnies with warm fussy fur, but underneath carry bloody claws and voracious drooling fangs of a cobra.

Obama is a delusional, childishly belligerent, immature, psychopathic liar over-compensates for his own pathetically abandoned and decimated self-image by strutting arrogantly through life on the coat tails, myths and financial support of those power hungry "Elitist" who brutally use him as a "puppet teleprompter reading battering ram" for their own freedom hating ends, and to destroy our Constitution. He knows no better; but "We the Sheeple" should have and would have, had the same people who own Barack Obama, the RNC and the DNC not also owned and controlled our ignorant, cowardly and gullibly deceitful mass media and the pathetically indoctrinated "Ivey League grads," who now take up space within it and dictate the corrupted changes now threatening our freedoms at a faster pace.

Barack Obama and his spoiled, churlish wife hate our country. She, as much as said so at the Democratic Convention when it was her turn to speak. They hate Constitutional principle and favor those of Marx and Engels. They have spent their lives learning to hate every principle the United States of America was founded upon. They have surrounded themselves with propagandized, leftist "morons," ignorant of history, ignorant of economics, ignorant regarding human decency, guided by extremely intelligent liberal educators, but all of whom fancy themselves "elitist intellectuals" (even the ignorant self-serving bureaucratic parasites). These pathetic elitists were groomed in the halcyon days of 1969's Students For a Democratic Society (SDS), in a drug using counter-culture society; its spawn, the Weathermen aka, Weather Underground Organization (WUO), the Black Panthers and other hallucinatory leftist groups, all members of a counter-culture revolution, who as Stalin and Mao believed, and all true Marxist were dedicated to the idea of imposing their own "rightness" and eliminating anyone who disagreed (yes, killing millions in USSR and China). The Weathermen openly discussed the necessity of having to eliminate 20,000,000 or so Americans (about 10% of the population at the time), who in their esteemed estimation would be incapable of "re-education". These same arrogant Marxist fools now inhabit the West Wing of our White House and are attempting to usurp your last bit of freedom. These parasites already control your income, your property, businesses, and your purchases by taxation, license, and permits. They also control your ability to travel, and limit your freedoms to useless and perverted laws totally, while passing laws to allow perverted sexual behavior.

We must respect "the office" we are told. Give him a little more time. I'll tell you what. Barack Hussein Obama and our Congress have had all the time this patriot is willing to give. When the office of the Presidency, the House of Representatives, the U.S. Senate and our Supreme Court are actively deceiving and working against the American people – not one iota of respect is earned or granted. I WILL NEVER RESPECT OR BOW TO DESTRUCTIVE, COLLECTIVIST LIES, NOR TO THEIR POWER, HOWEVER ATTAINED. I AM FORCED TO ADHERE TO THERE CORRUPTED AND PERVERTED LAWS OR FACE PRISON; OR BE KILLED (As what happened at Ruby Ridge, Waco, Kent State, Wounded Knee, and to Gordon Kahl).

I SAY, "IMPEACH OBAMA NOW!" VOTE ALL MEMBERS OF CONGRESS OUT THE NEXT ELECTION REGARDLESS OF PARTY. VOTE ALL SENATORS UP FOR RE-ELECTION OUT – GET RID OF THE REST OF THE GARBAGE AS THEIR TERMS COME UP. REDUCE CONGRESSIONAL SALARIES SO THAT SERVING YOUR COUNTRY IS A SACRIFICE AND AN HONOR, NOT AN EXPENSIVE GIFT AND A LICENSE TO STEAL (also, eliminate all tax funded retirement plans for elected officials and government employees, at both the Federal and State level). REPEAL THE 16TH AND 17TH AMENDMENTS. END THE FED. END THE IRS. END THE CRIMINAL SOCIAL SECURITY FRAUD. INSTITUTE THE FAIR TAX, WITH A CAP ON HOW MUCH WE CAN BE TAXED. FORCE THE FEDERAL GOVERNMENT TO BEG THE STATES FOR MONEY AND END ITS CONFISCATORY REIGN OF TERROR. DO THESE SIMPLE THINGS AND YOUR CHILDREN WILL BE FREE. FAIL AND YOU GET THE INDENTURED SERVITUDE WE HAVE IGNORANTLY BEEN VOTING FOR

Morals of Obama: "Personally, I believe Larry Sinclair's story and think Obama is bisexual. I think, like Keynes, Huxley, Frank, and others, he is compromised and enjoys sex with men; I feel that his immoral behavior and attitude is reflected in his decisions, including picking Kagan for a seat on the un-supreme court. I see no redeeming characteristics in this person. He is supported by ignorant blacks, who voted for him just because of being half black, homosexual, illegal's, and Marxist. As I stated, we are in trouble when 44% of the people think Obama is a "good President!" I feel Obama is nor fit to be President."

Chris Dodd
Career "criminal" Congressman Chris Dodd, schooled in homeopathic larceny by his own corrupt father has supported yet another scheme to rip off the American tax payer and strengthen his financial backers. "Career criminal" Dodd, known liar, has been professionally trained in the techniques of intubating automatic siphon hoses into the increasingly empty and cavernously hollow tax payer wallet.

"Criminal Dodd" is in excellent historical company. The single greatest financial fraud in history, "The Federal Reserve Act," made it possible for international "wanna be" wealth to become the world's undisputed financial oligarchy. The Federal Reserve Act gave illegal, unconstitutional access to American tax payer dollars by greedy private bank owners. This international, inbred financial slime, beholden to no nation under the sun, did not however, receive a guarantee of perpetual access to the wanton theft of American tax dollars. "Career criminal Dodd," bought and paid for decades ago will crown his corrupt career with as good a guarantee as 2,000 pages of unread colossal garbage can illegally provide when finally passed as consumer protection by our inept, treasonous Congress and signed into law by international banker's pet rock, Barack Hussein Obama.

The Federal Reserve Act, plotted in full at the nine-day, Jekyll Island meeting of 1910, finally misrepresented and bulled through Congress during the Christmas holiday was marketed to the gullible U.S. tax payer as protection against the international robber barons. We know now, of course, that the legislation was actually written by J.P. Morgan, Paul Warburg and several other international financiers for the express purpose of handing the U.S. money supply and financial future of America back to the Bank of England via the Rothschild family.

The Federal Reserve Act was a successful end run around the Constitutional Republic created by our Founders. It was the first major step in undermining the near fool proof governmental structure of the United States, which cleverly provided checks and balances making it nearly impossible to establish a "centralized government" or dictatorship. Added coups were the progressive income tax and Social Security, both incredible siphons for the transfer of wealth from the working middle class to the ultra rich. You might think that after 200-years and hundreds of millions starved, imprisoned, tortured, brutalized and murdered that the average person would begin to understand that socialism is not about sharing wealth; socialism is exclusively about controlling wealth. People still don't get it.

This international financial oligarchy developed a new concept of Communism, based on the political principles of Marx and Engels. The idea was to convert all world or national governments to a centralized form, whereby the "dictatorial leader" could easily be controlled by controlling that leader's purse strings (the currencies), and power. Literally all of today's social conflicts, such as the sexual revolution, feminism, gay rights, racism, class warfare, the dummying down of education, revisionist history, etc., etc. have been created, marketed and sold by this group, through the Communist Party to well intended, but easily duped Progressives for the purpose of undermining free market capitalism and promoting societal chaos. Keynesian economic theory was developed to lend credibility to this draconian, inhuman nonsense. Keynes, a sexual pervert, had little or no moral values, and those in the U.S., who have enjoined Keynesian economic theories, could care less about the stability of freedoms for the general populace. As a results of corrupting our currency, using "Keynesian system " by flooding the market with fiat money, we are in economic turmoil, and our political system has degenerated to a level that our government is controlled by a bunch of egotistical, power-hungry, money-grabbing dissipated rakehells.

Humans don't function well under chaos. The grandiose plan was for chaos to reach such a level that the average citizen would beg for relief. At this point, the oligarchs are poised and ready to step in with their centralized, collectivized government solution to save the day. Well, today is one of those days and criminal Dodd and friends have again lowered themselves to the occasion. Free markets and capitalism are blamed for the chaos, but today's dummied down victims of Progressive public education and redacted history do not understand that we have not seen free market capitalism since 1913 or so. Government regulation is the problem and government regulation is the answer we are provided, by the oligarchy to lock ourselves firmly into perpetual serfdom by our own choice and uneducated votes. It's a truly clever and insidious program and it is working to perfection – except maybe for the Tea Party, which, in my opinion, I feel will be captured by pseudo-conservatives of both parties!

Today, in 2010, nearly 100 years after the criminal passage of The Federal Reserve Act, again under the guise of consumer protection, (the same historical playbook) the international oligarchy's handpicked Obama Administration will finally hand the much desired "golden guarantee key" to the international banking oligarchy. Truly, an impressive coup for Chris; his father would be proud. Our country, however, is screwed (please pardon my crudeness).

Buried within this 2,000 page pile of unread, deceit, written by "we don't know who" are the long sought "permanent" tax payer subsidies, which guarantee that for the rest of time, the dummying down American tax payer will absorb 100% of all international banking risk, while sharing none of the profit with the very few private families, who slink quietly behind this legislative abortion.

With the additional soon to be, passing of illegal alien amnesty and some form of crap and tax, our once free American society will be permanently reduced to two classes of people; the ultra rich and their "economic slaves." The Obama Administration has been entrusted with the task of bringing to fruition the permanent indentured servitude of the American middle class. This was the dream conceived in 1773 by Mayer Amshel Bauer (Rothschild), Adam Weishaupt and their greedy, demented cronies.

Freedom is never given or granted. It is taken. Only vigilance can preserve it. Unfortunately, the American people have not been vigilant. Our children will pay for our mistake with their freedom. Remember this, when your kids ask "how did this happen?" You can tell them that in all fairness you were asked that the Obama Administration be given "just a little more time"... and what happened was time was given, valuable time, and by not acting, when we had one last chance, we lost our "freedoms."

One last word of caution! The Republicans will not save you. Republicans have become the second side of the same counterfeit coin. We no longer have a two-party system. We have a collusive sewer run beneath the boot heel of an international oligarchy. Think term limits. Think Independent. Think Tea Party. Ask yourself why John McCain never ran a real campaign?

Did Americans really have a vote? Of course not – but this can be changed by knowledge. Please educate yourself, and act prudently.

"Joe "Mr. Profanity himself, Biden"

One thing you can say about Ole Joe, he does not mind using the Lords name in vain. He has been caught more than once on national television cursing; using God in is disgusting cursing.

How can people be so stupid as to vote for this educated nut-case, Marxist? Hey, do not take my word for it, look at his voting record.

Regarding our Second Amendment under the Constitution.

He voted to keep assault weapons ban; and to close gun show loophole. (Apr 2007), I say, every patriotic American should be required to have an assault weapon in his home. According the Second Amendment, "the Right to Bear Arms."

Voted NO on prohibiting lawsuits against gun manufacturers. (Jul 2005): This "jerk" wants criminals to have the right to sue the manufacturer of guns if shot by a person protecting his family or property.

Voted NO on banning lawsuits against gun manufacturers for gun violence. (Mar 2004): See above

Voted YES on background checks at gun shows. (May 1999): I think we should take the guns away from Congress and the Courts, and do backgrounds check on them to determine if they are Marxist.

Voted NO on more penalties for gun & drug violations. (May 1999): Yes, ole Joe wants to protect the criminal while limiting citizens' rights to bear arms.

- Voted NO on loosening license & background checks at gun shows. (May 1999)

- Voted NO on maintaining current law: guns sold without trigger locks. (Jul 1998)

- Rated F by the NRA, indicating a pro-gun control voting record. (Dec 2003)

This guy is as dangerous as Obama, fortunately, he is not as articulate. He supports abortion, homosexual marriage, government bailouts, and Obama's health plan (euthanasia). In violation of the Constitution, he wants to give DC a seat in congress.

I do not know of one Marxist principle, Joe Biden does not support. To view his voting records go to: ontheissues.org/joe_biden_htm.

Barney "faggot" Frank

This guy should have been dismissed from office years ago on moral and ethic violations. Frank, one of the most corrupt politicians of our times is not only a Marxist, but also a pervert. He admitted running a homosexual sex ring from his office in 1989, but was excused because he suffered depression – WHAT? A congressman is allowed to break the law because he is depressed. The congressman wrote a misleading memo that went to a Virginia prosecutor and was aimed at ending Gobie's (Frank's male lover) probation on felony charges. It also found that 33 parking tickets issued to Frank's car, many when Gobie was driving were improperly waived through the congressman's House privileges. All of this and his Marxist view, but yet the stupid people of Massachusetts keeps voting him back into office. How many blacks, Marxist, and "queers" are there in his district? Hopefully, the people in Frank's district will wake up or at least become politically educated and realize how destructive this scumbag is to our Constitution.

In reality, they (all politicians and most bureaucrats) are all worthless parasites sucking the financial life blood out of productive individuals. I cannot think of any congressman that should be reelected, maybe, and just maybe there may be a few exceptions, like Ron Paul and I said maybe!

Side-bar: *Labor Union: The exploitation of the middle class worker:*

"Federal Labor Board Sanctions Union Boss Deception"

Thu, 06/04/2009 - 18:12 — Nick Cote

As if there was ever any doubt about whether or not the federal government favors union bosses over individual employees (including union members and nonmembers alike), the National Labor Relations Board last week determined that union bosses may lie to employees about employers' contract proposals.

In a Division of Advice memorandum, NLRB Associate General Counsel Barry Kearney ruled that union chiefs do not commit an unfair labor practice when they misstate the details of a contract proposed by the company.

In the NLRB's twisted logic, union bosses can deceive the very employees it has the duty to fairly represent so long as the deception involves "wholly an internal union matter."

This is a textbook example showing just why Right to Work protections are so needed. In 22 states with Right to Work laws, employees cannot be forced to join or pay dues to a union to get or keep a job. When "representatives" deliberately lie to employees about contract negotiations, why should workers should be forced to pay for this "service".

You may be misled into thinking that trade unions are for the benefit of the working class, but it is not. The unions are nothing more than a tool of the "Elitist," using members to keep corrupted and compromised politician in office to make sure that the Elitist agenda is fulfilled. The only time trade unions represented the average working person was that time before mobsters, corrupted politicians, and corrupted union organizers conspired to gain control all unions. Had those "capitalist" that were privileged to engage in the free enterprise system acted fairly and provided safe working conditions, fair wages, and benefits instead of yielding to their desires of greed and power, unions would have never been necessary...... now, many are caught, like most of the middle class, in a position of relying on the Power Elite for our existence, as it is they who control our fiat currencies, control our political systems that engages our sons and daughters in winless and indefinable wars, and determines the future of our children. I want them out of control, and our freedoms restored. I pray for the restoration of moral values, a return to Constitutional law, equally applied to all men, and freed of all taxation, except what was provided by the "Organic Constitution." I want the privilege of owning my property, not renting it from the government, via a property tax. I want control of my earnings, without greedy politicians taking a portion of what I earn for their own self-serving interest, or redistributing my hard earned money to unproductive people. God Save America! – **"End of side bar"**

Our government has become "our master," rather than "our servant," in turn individual accountability and responsibility of elected officials has diminished as a rapid pace. We are no longer living in the conventional flesh and blood universe, in which actions and behavior have consequences, and wanting a thing means having to go out and work for it. We are now a part of a "global community." We are (and I do mean "We") a member of the New World Order. It takes a village to raise us, an idiot's village of bureaucrats, academics, politicians, assorted officials and union members to lead us to our own "political and economic death." We are a collective society, and have only one remaining right, the right to be collectively stupid.

I do not know one Congressman or member of Obana's staff, who has not supported Marxist's principles. We have a President's Cabinet made up of progressives promoting globalization and looking to enhance its own power and wealth. Clinton, and most of the rest are nothing more than members of the Establishment;" seeking to destroy our free enterprise system. She and her husband are members of the CFR and neither has really answered truthfully about Vince Foster's death, Whitewater (my opinion), or most of the controversial questions surrounding their time in the White Hous; we can't get the truth, as the files are sealed.

Speaking of the Clintons, let have a look (**another side-bar**): A careful study of the Clintons reveals a long list of associating with "Criminals – Here are a few:

Jorge Cabrera, a convicted felon from Florida, gave the DNC $20,000 and then attended a political reception in Miami at which Cabrera got his picture taken with Al Gore. Cabrera was soon invited to a December 1995 pre-Christmas event at the White House and was photographed with First Lady Hillary Rodham Clinton. The next month in January 1996, undercover agents arrested Cabrera with three tons of Colombian cocaine. Prior to Cabrera's January arrest, he had been arrested twice on drug charges, and pleaded guilty to non-drug-related charges in both cases. Cabrera is serving a 19-year prison sentence. (The Detroit News, 2/16/97; Miami Herald, 1/19/97; The Washington Post, 10/20/96)

Yah Lin "Charlie" Trie, President Clinton's longtime friend and a Democratic fund-raiser, was at the center of the 1996 United States <u>campaign finance controversy</u> and eventually pleaded guilty to two charges in his Arkansas trial (May 21, 1999). Trie plead guilty to a felony charge of causing false statements and a misdemeanor count of making political contributions in the names of others.

It was Charlie Trie who arranged for international Chinese weapons dealer, Wang Jun, chairman of CITIC, the chief investment arm of the PRC, and Poly Technologies (a "front company for the PRC military") to meet with Mr. Clinton at a Democrat Party event at the White House on Feb. 6, 1996. CITIC Ka Wah Bank includes 28 branches in Hong Kong, a branch in Macau, a branch in Shanghai and its PRC-incorporated wholly-owned subsidiary, CITIC Ka Wah Bank (China) Limited, which is headquartered in Shenzhen with branches in Shanghai and Beijing. The Bank also has branches in New York and Los Angeles.

At the time Clinton met with Wang, the Bureau of Alcohol, Tobacco and Firearms and the Customs Service were wrapping up an investigation which caught Wang's company smuggling at least $4 million worth of 2,000 illegal AK-47 assault weapons destined for gang members in California. President Clinton later admitted Wang's attendance at the White House was "clearly inappropriate."

Grigory Loutchansky, linked by Interpol to the Russian mafia, money laundering, drug trafficking, nuclear smuggling across the Baltics, and international arms trading, attended a Democrat Party White House dinner in October of 1993. Loutchansky got a private two-minute meeting and a picture with Mr. Clinton. (The Washington Times, 2/11/97; The Detroit News, 2/16/97; New York Post, 11/1/96; Time, 7/8/96) Loutchansky was invited back to a second DNC dinner in July 1995. A year before, Canada had blocked Loutchansky from entering Canada because he had failed a background check. Canadian officials also had questions about the source of Loutchansky's Nordex company's assets. (The Washington Times, 3/1/97) Both of Clinton's CIA Directors James Woolsey and John Deutch described Loutchansky's Nordex company as an "organization associated with Russian criminal activity."

Eric Wynn: A Clinton "cronie" that benefited a member of the Bonanno organized crime family and who served two years in prison for theft and tax charges, attended a December 1995 White House coffee with Clinton. In 1996, Wynn attended four other DNC fund-raising events involving Clinton. Wynn has been arrested five times during a six months period while out on bail for aggravated assault on a police officer, resisting arrest, aggravated assault with a motor vehicle, violation of a restraining order, terroristic threats and driving while intoxicated. At least one of the arrests occurred between DNC fund-raisers Wynn attended in 1996 with Clinton. (The Detroit News, 2/16/97; The Washington Post, 2/20/97; The Star-Ledger, 2/20/97)

Roger Tamraz, an international fugitive from Interpol, donated $177,000 to Democrats and the DNC through his companies and attended several White House dinners and coffees in 1995-1996. Tamraz is a former financier wanted, according to a 1989 Interpol warrant, in Lebanon for embezzling $200 million from his failed bank. On June 2, 1995, Tamraz was briefed by a National Security Council (NSC) expert on Russia at the same time he was negotiating a multibillion-dollar deal to build a pipeline from oil reserves from the Caspian Sea to Turkey through Azerbaijan and Armenia. On July 26, Tamraz contributed $20,000 to the DNC. After the meeting occurred, then-DNC Party Chairman Don Fowler called an NSC official to try to overturn a recommendation that Tamraz not attend high-level White House meetings. Tamraz went on to attend four more White House events with Clinton which included receptions, dinners and the premiere of the movie "Independence Day." Tamraz, through his New York-based oil company, gave $50,000 to the DNC after going to a DNC sponsored White House reception on Sept. 11, 1995, and a dinner four days later. In October, Tamraz contributed another $100,000 at the direction of the DNC to the Virginia Democrat Party using his Tamoil Inc., company. Tamraz also had coffee with Gore on Oct. 5, 1995, and with Clinton on April 1, 1996.

Russ Barakat, a south Florida Democrat Party official, was indicted on criminal charges just five days after his coffee meeting at the White House in April 1995. Ultimately, Barakat was convicted for tax evasion. A Florida newspaper was full of stories about Barakat's problems with the law before his White House visit, but he was asked in for coffee anyway.

Norman Hsu, former Democratic fundraiser, was sentenced to more than 24 years in prison in 2009 by a judge who accused him of funding his fraud by manipulating the political process in a way that 'strikes at the very core of our democracy.' U.S. District Judge Victor Marrero sentenced the 58-year-old Hsu, who raised money for Hillary Rodham Clinton and others, to 20 years in prison for his guilty plea to fraud charges and another four years and four months in prison for his conviction at trial for breaking campaign finance laws.

Chung Lo contributed $10,300 to the DNC. The bulk of the money was given in July 1996, the same month Ms. Lo was arrested on 14 counts of bank and mortgage fraud. Lo's arrest came four days before she was to host a $400,000 Asian American fund-raiser featuring Clinton. The event was abruptly canceled. Lo was convicted of tax evasion in the 1980s under the name of Esther Chu. Lo had attended a White House coffee and a fund-raising event involving First Lady Hillary Rodham Clinton and Vice President Gore.

Kim Weissman writes in a Congress Action update on July 13, 1997,

"One of the many troubling aspects of this affair is how the cesspool of corruption which the Clintons brought to Washington can cause even the most honorable men to prostitute their principles, attempting to defend the indefensible.

John Glenn was an honorable man, a true American hero. A Marine, one of America's first astronauts, the first American to ride a rocket into earth orbit at a time when our rockets had the nasty habit of routinely blowing up in people's faces. His bravery, his patriotism, his honor were above reproach and beyond question; until Bill Clinton came to town. And in a few short years this bona fide hero has transformed himself into nothing more than a party hack, in service to monumental presidential corruption. Once a man throws his honor on the trash heap, it can never be reclaimed. And Glenn is not alone among democrats compromising their integrity to protect Bill Clinton. As for the media, which has instituted a virtual news blackout in which live coverage is nonexistent and then whines that nobody cares, which ignores crimes, espionage, and possible treason, and shamelessly peddles the democrat line that "the system is broken", their ethics and principles in this matter are beneath contempt. As usual. The media see these hearings as their chance to enact "reform" which will enhance their power even further, and subversion of our government and treason in high office is of no interest. The integrity of our government and safety of the nation ranks below their self-aggrandizement."

Clinton's Criminal Appointees

Attorney General **Janet Reno** fabricated charges of child molestation against the Branch Davidians in Waco, Texas, ordering the **use of military equipment and the use of chemical agents** against citizens of the United States. Eighty-six men, women, and children died after FBI agents used grenade launchers to mount a CS gas attack on their compound. Larry Potts—who coordinated the Waco raid and was censured for his role in the 1992 Ruby Ridge, Idaho, shoot-out -- was promoted to deputy director of the FBI by Reno.

It was revealed in 2010 by Dick Morris, a longtime friend of Clinton and political advisor during his first term in office, that Janet Reno essentially blackmailed Bill Clinton to re-appoint her to a second term as Attorney General.

He told Sean Hannity that the President was not going to appoint Attorney General Janet Reno to a second term in office following the federal barrage on the Branch Davidian ranch at Mount Carmel.

"Bill Clinton orchestrated that takeover and in fact was so ashamed of what he did in Waco that he was not going to appoint Janet Reno to a second four year term" Morris stated. "She told him in a meeting right before the inauguration day for his new term, that 'if you don't appoint me, I'm gonna tell the truth about Waco' and that forced Clinton's hand in reappointing her."

Washington lawyer, Clinton confidant and golfing partner, **Vernon Jordan**, was deposed by Ken Starr for his role in obtaining $50,000 in "consulting fees" for Webster Hubbell, between the time Hubbell left the Justice Department and entered federal prison. Starr was trying to determine if those fees were **"hush money."** That money came from Revlon Corporation, where Mr. Jordan sits on the board of directors. Jordan, at the request of Clinton's personal secretary, Betty Currie, had also helped Monica Lewinsky search for a new job and a lawyer after she left the White House.

Vernon Jordan's relationship with Bill Clinton goes back to a 1991 Bilderberger meeting where Clinton was introduced to the group by Jordan. The <u>Bilderbergers</u> arrogantly plot the subversion and silent takeover of constitutional governments everywhere. Their goal is a <u>World Government</u> run exclusively by their hand-picked puppets. It was shortly after attending the 1991 Bilderberger meeting, Governor Bill Clinton was selected to be the next President of the United States.

President Clinton has done a masterful job of placing "fall-guys" between himself and his administration's indigenous corruption scandals. Independent Counsels have indicted and jailed senior administration officials for corruption, but Mr. Clinton has always maintained arms-length plausible deniability. Clinton's defensive modus operandi: admit nothing, deny everything and make counter allegations.

It was alleged **George Stephanopoulos**, Senior Advisor, took a $600,000 loan below market interest and with insufficient collateral from NationsBank, a bank having business before the Clinton Administration, lied to Congress during Whitewater hearings, and attempted to have Whitewater investigator Jay Stephens at the RTC fired.

Secretary of Labor, **Robert Reich** lied to Congress when he wrote that there were no memos circulating in the Labor Department instructing staff to gather political material against the Contract with America. Such memos were later published. This did not matter, as the Contract with America was the "brain-child" of CFR member, Newt Gingrich, and was a sham..

On Feb. 12, 1995, the Los Angeles Times reveals Veterans Affairs Secretary **Jesse Brown** made 20 trips at taxpayers' expense to his hometown of Chicago—rarely attending any official events.

Former Secretary of Defense, **Les Aspin**, through criminal negligence was responsible for the death of Army Rangers in Somalia. He has never been held accountable in public hearings. He subsequently resigned and is now deceased.

The Los Angeles Times revealed on June 25, '95, Energy Secretary **Hazel O'Leary**, at taxpayers' expense, routinely upgrades her airline flights to business and first class and stays at expensive hotels—seeking reimbursement from the government at as much as 150 percent of the maximum level allowed. In Jan. '96, the General Accounting Office audit finds $255,000 in undocumented expenses from **Hazel O'Leary's** trips abroad. In April, '96, a General Accounting Office audit showed that the 14 overseas trips Energy Secretary Hazel O'Leary took in 1994 and 1995 netted only about $448 million worth of business -- not the $2 billion her administration claimed -- and that some of the deals concluded on the trips benefitted foreign firms more than U.S. companies. An Energy Department inspector general report stated that part of the $4.6 million **Secretary Hazel O'Leary** spent on overseas trips may have been spent illegally.

Chief of Staff to the First Lady, **Margaret Williams** obstructed justice when she removed documents from the office of Vince Foster. She lied to Congress about removing those documents.

Treasury Department Employee, **Joshua Steiner**, lied to Congress about conversations with White House personnel about the RTC and has resigned.

Former Chief of Staff, **Mack McLarty** conspired with Democratic Congressional Leadership to block access to vital documents in a Congressional hearing.

USIA Inspector General, **Marian Benett**, covered up credit-card fraud by USIA Inspector General staff.

Federico Pena, Secretary of Transportation has been accused of awarding State and federal contracts to companies in which he had a financial interest.

Assistant Attorney General for Civil Rights, **Deval Patrick** was accused of using extortion to force banks to give preferential treatment to minorities.

(The above information regarding the Clintons was taken from the Internet)

Do you understand why I am concerned enough to place myself in jeopardy by writing this book. If, by chance, enough people will read what I have written and get politiclly involved, we can make a difference; however, you must be aware of the consequences I face by simply printing the truth and expressing my opinion. I have subjected myself to ridicule, and possibly prosecution for stating my opinions and stating the truth.

Mine is not the first book attempting to expose the "International Financial Cartel," or the illegal actions of our government. Lyndon

LaRouche was arrested for writing and speaking out against the same type of corruption in 1988 on, what I believed to be trumped-up charges. He was sentenced to 15 years' for conspiracy to commit mail fraud and tax code violations. Anyone who has ever read any parts of the Tax Code understands that this Regulation was written subjectively and is interpreted by the same bureaucrats who enforce this so-called tax law.

LaRouche, and his followers were a threat to the Establishment, and it is dangerous to be an enemy of this group of Elitist. If my book (this book) get the least bit of national attention, I may not live very long, or could face charges (Criminal or Civil) to shut me down and discredit anything I have written.

Now, look at the death of Foster (more about Clinton):

THE EVENTS SURROUNDING THE DEATH OF VINCENT FOSTER (also taken from the Internet)
On July 20, 1993, six months to the day after Bill Clinton took office as President of the United States, the White House Deputy Council, Vincent Foster, told his secretary Deborah Gorham, "I'll be right back". He then walked out of his office, after offering his co-worker <u>Linda Tripp</u>, the leftover M&Ms from his lunch tray.

That was the last time Vincent Foster was seen alive.

Contrary to the White House spin, Vincent Foster's connection to the Clinton's was primarily via Hillary, rather than Bill. Vincent and Hillary had been partners together at the rose law firm, and allegations of an <u>ongoing affair</u> had persisted from the Little Rock days to the White House itself.

Vincent Foster had been struggling with the Presidential Blind trust. Normally a trivial matter, the trust had been delayed for almost 6 months and the U.S. trustee's office was beginning to make noises about it. Foster was also the keeper of the files of the Clinton's Arkansas dealings and had <u>indicated in a written memo</u> that "Whitewater is a can of worms that you should NOT open!"

But Vincent's position at the White House did not sit well with him. Only days before, following a public speech stressing the value of

personal integrity, he had confided in friends and family that he was thinking of resigning his position. Foster had even written an outline for his letter of resignation, thought by this writer to have been used as the center portion of the fake "suicide note". Foster had scheduled a private meeting with Bill Clinton for the very next day, July 21, 1993 at which it appeared Foster intended to resign.

Vincent Foster had spent the morning making "busy work" in his office and had been in attendance at the White House announcement of Louis Freeh as the new head of the FBI earlier in the day (passing by the checkpoint manned by White House uniformed guard Styles).

This is a key point. The White House is the most secure private residence in the world, equipped with a sophisticated entry control system and video surveillance system installed by the Mitre Corporation. Yet no record exist that Vincent Foster left the White House under his own power on July 20th, 1993. No video of him exiting the building exists. No logbook entry shows he checked out of the White House.

Several hours after he was last seen inside the White House, Vincent Foster was found dead in Fort Marcy Park, in a Virginia suburb just outside Washington D.C.

The death was ruled a suicide (the first major Washington suicide since Secretary of Defense James Forrestal in 1949), but almost immediately rumors began to circulate that the story of a suicide was just a cover-up for something much worse.

The first witness to find the body insisted that there had been no gun near the body. The memory in Foster's pager had been erased. Critical evidence began to vanish. Many witnesses were harassed. Others were simply ignored. There were even suggestions that the body had been moved, and a Secret Service memo surfaced which reported that Foster's body had been found in his car! The official reports were self-contradictory. The Looting of Foster's office: While the U.S. Park Police (a unit not equipped for a proper homicide investigation) studied the body, Foster's office at the White House was being looted. Secret Service agent Henry O' Neill watched as Hillary Clinton's chief of staff, Margaret Williams, carried boxes of papers out of Vincent Foster's office before the Park Police showed up to seal it. Amazing when you consider that the official identification of Vincent Foster's body by Craig Livingstone did not take place until 10PM! Speaking of Craig Livingstone, another Secret Serviceman saw him remove items from Vincent Foster's office in violation of the official seal. Witnesses also saw Bernard Nussbaum in Foster's office as well. Three witnesses noted that Patsy Thomason (sister to Robert, who was involved with Spyro and me in dealing with Libya, later discussed in this book), director of the White House's Office of Administration, was desperate to find the combination to Vincent Foster's safe. Ms. Thomason finally opened the safe, apparently with the help of a special "MIG" technical team signed into the White House in the late hours. Two envelopes reported to be in the safe by Foster's secretary Deborah Gorham, addressed to Janet Reno and to William Kennedy III, were never seen again. When asked the next day regarding rumors of the safe opening, Mack McLarty told reporters Foster's office did not even have a safe, a claim immediately shot down by former occupants of that office.

The next day, when the Park Police arrived for the official search of Vincent Foster's office, they were shocked to learn that Nussbaum, Thomason and Williams had entered the office. Conflicts channeled through Janet Reno's Department of Justice resulted in the Park Police merely sitting outside Foster's office while Bernard Nussbaum continued his own search of Foster's office. During this search, he opened and upended Vincent Foster's briefcase, showing it to be empty. Three days later, it would be claimed that this same briefcase was where the torn up suicide note was discovered.

The boxes of documents removed from Foster's office by Hillary Clinton's chief of staff, Margaret Williams, were taken to the private residence area of the White House! Eventually, only 54 pages emerged.

One set of billing records, under subpoena for two years, and thought to have originated in Foster's office, turned up unexpectedly in the private quarters of the White House, with Hillary's fingerprints on them!

So, who ordered the office looting?

Bill Clinton was unavailable, being on camera with Larry King. But Hillary Clinton, who had only the day before diverted her planned return to Washington D.C. to Little Rock, was on the phone from

Little Rock to someone at the White House in the moments before the looting took place.

The initial reactions: Back in Little Rock, Foster's friends weren't buying it. Doug Buford, friend and attorney, stated, "...something was badly askew." Foster's brother-in-law, a former congressman, also did not accept that depression was what had been behind the "suicide": "That's a bunch of crap." And Webster Hubbell, former Clinton deputy attorney general, phoned a mutual friend to say, "Don't believe a word you hear. It was not suicide. It couldn't have been."

Outside experts not connected the official investigation also had their doubts.

Vincent J. Scalise, a former NYC detective, Fred Santucci, a former forensic photographer for NYC, and Richard Saferstein, former head of the New Jersey State Crime Lab formed a team and did an investigation of the VWF case for the Western Journalism Center of Fair Oaks, Calif. They arrived at several conclusions:

(1) Homicide cannot and should not be ruled out.

(2) The position of the arms and legs of the corpse were drastically inconsistent with suicide.

(3) Neither of VWF's hand was on the handgrip when it was fired. This is also inconsistent with suicide. The investigators noted that in their 50 years of combined experience they had "never seen a weapon or gun positioned in a suicide's hand in such an orderly fashion."

(4) VWF's body was probably in contact with one or more carpets prior to his death. The team was amazed that the carpet in the trunk of VF's care had not been studied to see whether he had been carried to the park in the trunk of his own car.

(5) The force of the gun's discharge probably knocked VF's glasses flying; however, it is "inconceivable" that they could have traveled 13 feet through foliage to the site where they were found; ergo, the scene probably was tampered with.

(6) The lack of blood and brain tissue at the site suggests VF was carried to the scene. The peculiar tracking pattern of the blood on his right cheek also suggests that he was moved.

Despite numerous official assurances that Vincent Foster really did commit suicide, more and more Americans, <u>over 70%</u> at the last count, no longer believe the official story. TV specials, most notably the one put out by A&E's "Inside Investigations" with Bill Kurtis, have failed to answer the lingering questions, indeed have engaged in deliberate fraud to try to dismiss the evidence that points to a cover-up. (Source: Internet)

During a lunch meeting with Mark Middleton, an assistant to Clinton, told Larry Wallace (lobbyist with whom I was associated in early 90's) and me that the secret service "caught Hillary and Vince on the floor of her office having sex….. (I doubt if Mark or Larry will admit to this conversation, but I will take a polygraph test to prove that I am telling the truth. ----**END OF SIDE-BAR!**)

What I have written is an example of the kind of people controlling the fate of our nation. The Bush family was no better (do your own research about Prescott Bush and Bush's support of "The New World Order).

Now, we are familiar with some of the past actons to lead us into a global political system by both the Clintons and Bush, and with a pro-Muslim, Marxist, Obama. Let's continue looking at Obama's cronies.

Eric Holder: Attorney General Eric Holder is more interested in bullying Arizonians over immigration enforcement than in protecting Americans from nuclear, biological or chemical weapons. He is a joke and a progressive. However, it is my opinion, that nothing happens unless planned by the PE.

More on Obama's appointees (Some of the following was taken from the Internet, entitled, "Obama's Socialist Appointees - Where is the Spotlight? New Zeal, Obama File 87 –By Trevor Loundon")

Published by I.O. along with other articles by one whose research has been fundamental to exposing Barack Obama and the global movement, of which he is a key component. The Supreme Court is packed with political appointees. Any reasonable person can read the Constitution and plainly see these political cronies violate the Constitution in their rulings.

First, let's now have a look at Obama's association with the Democratic Socialists of America (DSA). I, in fact, think this organization should be called "Marxist Militants of America."

Here is what "Loundon" states about Obama's association with the DSA: "President Obama has close personal and political ties to several DSA members including Quentin Young, Timuel Black, the late Rabbi Arnold Jacob Wolf, the late Saul Mendelson, Lou Pardo, Congressman Danny Davis and DSA honorees Jackie Grimshaw, Jackie Kendall and Congresswoman Jan Schakowsky."

According to the article, "DSA's several thousand strong membership has grown incresingly militant over the years until the point its policies are almost indistinguishable from those of the Communist Party USA."

In an article in DSA's "<u>Democratic Left, Spring 2007</u>," DSA National Political Committee member David Green wrote;

Our goal as socialists is to abolish private ownership of the means of production. Our immediate task is to limit the capitalist class's prerogatives in the workplace...

In the short run we must at least minimize the degree of exploitation of workers by capitalists. We can accomplish this by promoting full employment policies, passing local living wage laws, but most of all by increasing the union movement's power...

"DSA has some cross membership with the Communist Party and considerable cross-membership with the equally militant Committees of Correspondence for Democracy and Socialism."

Congressman are associated with the DSA, including John Conyers, Danny Davis, Jan Schakowsky (all close Obama supporters) Jerrold Nadler, Bob Filner, Maxine Waters, and many others, Is it any wonder that the principles of Marx and Engels are so entrenched in our political system?

DSA has key personnel or allies at the top of AFL-CIO, SEIU, United Auto Workers, United Steelworkers of America and other major unions.

Most union members are unknowingly supporting Marxism by belonging to unions controlled and managed by Marxist.

It is a known fact that DSA has considerable influence in ACORN, ADA, ACLU, Working Families Party, Green Party, Democratic Party, US Action, Jobs with Justice, Economic Policy Institute, Campaign for America's Future, Demos (which Obama helped found), Black Radical Congress, Black Panthers, and many other mass organizations, including some churches."

Former DSA National Political Committee member Kurt Stand is currently serving a 17 year jail sentence for spying for the former East Germany and offering to spy for the South African Communist Party. His wife and co-conspirator Theresa Squillacote, a former Pentagon lawyer and a Committees of Correspondence member is serving 22 years..

Do you think DSA is harmless, insignificant? Next I list several members of the Obama administration who have had some ties to DSA/Socialist international- ranging from paid up DSA membership, to signing a DSA petition, to addressing one DSA sponsored event, to being related to a DSA member.

Some may be entirely innocent, but some may not. The Question is Do any, or all warrant further investigation? judge. These are found on the Internet.

"Ron Bloom - Manufacturing Czar is a socialist since his teens, has worked for several DSA linked organizations including SEIU, Jewish Labor Committee and United Steelworkers of America.

David Bonior - Member of the Obama Economic Transition Team-now delegated by president Obama to negotiate the unification of the AFL-CIO and Change to Win labor federations. Former Democratic speaker of the house David Bonior, has been linked to DSA for many years and had formally joined the organization by 2006.

Rosa Brooks - Senior advisor to the Under Secretary of Defense for Policy, Michele Flournoy. Reportedly named after communist radical Rosa Luxemburg, Brooks is the daughter of prominent DSA member, Movement for a Democratic Society board member and Progressives for Obama founder, Barbara Ehrenreich. Rosa Brooks is a well known "liberal" newspaper columnist and writer on defense and international relations. Brooks has served as Special Counsel to the President at George Soros' Open Society Institute.

Carol Browner - Energy Czar/Director of the White House Office of Energy and Climate Change Policy. Until summer 2008 <u>Carol Browner</u> was a member of Socialist International Commission for a Sustainable World Society." - **End of Quote** -

OBAMA'S choice for a Supreme Court Justice: Elena Kagan is a Marxist. Do not take my word for it read her Thesis, "TO THE FINAL CONFLICT: SOCIALISM IN NEW YORK CITY, 1900-1933" - By: ELENA KAGAN -April **15,** 1981; "A senior thesis submitted to the History Department of Princeton University in partial fulfillment of the requirements for the degree of Bachelor of Art TO MY PARENTS Acknowledgments" – not the first or only Marxist appointed to the Court. Too bad "conservative" congressman had the "guts" to stand up and call her what she is, a "Communist." No Senator stood up to "filibuster" her nomination --- wonder why? Are they all compromised? Where are you Senators, "Shelby, and Sessions?"

There are so many more appointees, who are "Marxist," most you already know about, but maybe not, have you heard of Obama's former homosexual (or bisexual) lover (mentioned earlier in this book), Larry Sinclair? Sinclair's reputation and creditability had been tarnished by the establishment, so, do not expect the media, including FOX to provide much information regarding Sinclair and Jones, another one of Obama's past homosexual lovers (Jones died a suspicious death, "The infamous Rev, Wright," may have been involved in a cover-up; read Sinclair's book and decide for yourself). I believe Sinclair, as I know Obama to be a liar, as well as his VP.

And of course there are those behind the scenes, that most of us do not know, so powerful, that their names are never spoken in the media, connecting them to the political or economic world, but they are there, and in control.

The government agencies mentioned is, for the most part, worthless and are parasites who feed on productive people. When governments and government agencies are given the ability to set their own parameters, they increase in size and authority rather than decrease it. If you let an animal loose in a paddock full of food, it will eat until it bursts. Individually, most people are smarter than that, collectively they're not. These agencies "eat like animals."

In my opinion there are cultures, races, and just irresponsible people who live for the here and now and innately are not motivated to look at the future for what is best for our nation. They vote, based on race, religion, and/or what the government will give them immediately. We think we have a Democracy (was not the intent, as we wore founded as a Republic), which, if true, will eventually leads to tyranny, but they do not get it. There is more to a freedom than a "privilege to vote scheme;" there is the rule of Constitutional law, which is now ignored by the courts, bureaucrats, and the government in general... It is not the freedom for everyone to vote that defines a free nation, but the freedom for people who cannot monetarily benefit from the outcome of an election to vote. Voters should be qualified. Once, votes can be bought by promises of special treatments and those who are parasites on society, and are in the majority, freedoms are doomed.

Collective stupidity is the results of a lack of individual responsibility and accountability

Collective stupidity is the product of a lack of individual responsibility and accountability. That is why mobs will do things that the individuals in that mob would not do. Mob rule and not the rule of law; it causes lynching's, civil disobedience, and corrupt politics. It is why a committee will produce results, regulations and laws so ridiculous that no individual in that committee alone would have produced. It is why legislatures during an economic crisis will vote themselves raises, and increase spending, such as voting for TARP. Because there is no individual point of accountability, bureaucrats can hide behind committees and majority rule, and ignore the Constitution... A collective group in that way can be less humane and less compassionate, than an individual. A mob can be emotionally aroused to kill, mane, and destroy the rule of law; such as riots, and destruction of private property by groups of lawless people. We are confronted with a challenge to preserve individualism and to fight against collectivism.

You must remember that history does not occur by accident, as we are led to believe by the pseudo-conservative talking-heads on TV. There are those who scheme to make history. The "schemers" have an agenda; they are an international cartel plotting to control the worlds resources.. Washington is only one place of many, these amoral rascals control and enforce their will to bring the U.S. into "The New World Order." Allow me to quote Quigley to prove my claim, **Carroll Quigley, Georgetown University history professor (deceased), in Tragedy and Hope: A History of the World in Our Time, 1966, made this claim:**

"There does exist and has existed for a generation, an international Anglophile network which operates, to some extent, in the way the radical Right believes the Communists act. In fact, this network, which we may identify as the Round Table groups, has no aversion to cooperating with the Communists, or any other groups, and frequently does so. I know of the operations of this network because I have studied it for 20 years and was permitted for two years, in the early 1960s, to examine its papers and secret record. "In addition to these pragmatic goals, the powers of financial capitalism had another far-reaching aim, nothing less than to create a world system of financial control in private hands able to dominate the political system of each country and the economy of the world as a whole. This system was to be controlled in a feudalist fashion by the central banks of the world acting in concert, by secret agreements arrived at in frequent private meetings and conferences. The apex of the system was the Bank for International Settlements in Basle, Switzerland; a private bank owned and controlled by the world's central banks which are private corporations. The growth of financial capitalism made possible a centralization of world economic control and use of this power for the direct benefit of financiers and the indirect injury of all other economic groups." A private bank owned and controlled by the insiders."

"America is today the leader of a world-wide anti-revolutionary movement in the defense of vested interests. She now stands for what Rome stood for: Rome consistently supported the rich against the poor . . . and since the poor, so far, have always and everywhere been far more numerous than the rich, Rome's policy made for inequality, for injustice, and for the least happiness of the greatest number." -----

As I see it, the great contribution which Dr. Carroll Quigley unintentionally made by writing Tragedy and Hope was to help the informed person realize the utter contempt which the Power Elite have for ordinary people. Human beings are treated "en masse" as helpless sheep in a slaughterhouse where "the shepherd" of economic and political power subject them to wars, revolution, civil strife, taxation, fiat currency, confiscation, subversion, indoctrination, manipulation and outright deception as it suits their fancy in their destructive schemes for world domination. The only enemy these internationalist parasites face is the middle class, and people who want to remain free... There is the constant fear that the masses might awaken and frustrate their gigantic schemes, particularly where they have acquired an education and accumulated a little property (which gives them a highly significant degree of independence).

That is what has happened to the mass of humanity in America, up until recent years. They constituted the great and overwhelming majority of the people, called the middle class. And Dr. Quigley, as we have already seen, leaves no doubt as to the menace which middle-class Americans are believed to represent insofar as the Establishment is concerned. This is why we have witnessed a planned dummying down in our educational system, and a scheme to distract us from political issues and history by use of a controlled media and entertainment industry, including attention and great emphasis on sports. Most men knows more about their favorite sports team than they know about current pending legislation in Congress that will have a lasting effect on their lives, and women had rather watch their favorite "soaps" than learn about the history of our lost Republic.

It was once the great American dream to make as many people as possible a part of the great middle class because it was recognized to be the foundation of our society and the most important segment of the population, in maintaining a moral, self-governing, secure, and freedom-loving people. But, obviously, if you are trying to set up a virtual global dictatorship, this group is the enemy. This group will resist a dictatorship. At least, it will do so, if it knows what is happening. So, this is the fact of life which the super-rich collectivists of the Establishment faced and has addressed with a plan to destroy the middle class, by corrupting politicians, "changing history," and diminishing moral values. Everything they do must be accomplished in an atmosphere of hidden agendas, secret political meetings, propaganda and deception. Otherwise they keep running into a strong resentment and resistance when they try to compel middle class Americans to give up their freedoms, independence, their property, and their constitutional prerogatives. The problem we face is that the Power Elitist is winning, as the dummying down "technique injections" of the PE are taking effect.

Perhaps it is time for Congress to consider legislation that allows our law enforcement authorities and courts to deal decisively with those who preach the overthrow of our government and the replacement of our Constitution with any form of totalitarianism - Communism, National Socialism, Fascism and Sharia. We cannot afford to remain blind to these organizations and their membership. On the other-hand, I do not trust Congress to write a law which would punish our true enemy, "The Elitist," as we, the true believers in our Constitution may be the target and the government may come after us, if such law was passed, claiming that it is we who want to overthrow the government…. something to consider!!

NOW, WHO IS MORE DANGEROUS, THE ENEMY IN THE MIDDLE EAST OR THE ENEMY IN D.C.? ----- GOD HELP US!

CHAPTER EIGHT: RACE RELATION, SOCIAL ISSUES, GOVENEMENT, AND MEDIA "CRAP" - IN GENERAL

I know that many may call me a racist, and anti-Semitic, based on portions of this book taken out of context, but I am neither and I am able to support everything written, as facts, with facts. I have not failed to state when I am expressing opinions.

My statements about Obama are not racist, as my views are based on the truths and observations. For the record, I supported Alan Keyes in his bid for the Republican Party's nomination, and, as far as being against Jews, it is stupid for anyone to make the claim that I am anti-Semitic, as my grandfather was a Jew. My family name was Braun, which was derived from the family of Braunschwieg, in Stuttgart, Germany. In about 1760, the Germans wanted Jewish names changed to make the sound more German, thus the name Braunschwieg was changed to Braun (also, the names Graft, Beck, and other last names may to traced back to Braunschwieg).

If a decision must be made about who is to survive in the Middle East, I side with the Jews. Israel is to be protected at all cost, even if it means worldwide nuclear war, and worldwide destruction. I believe that we are God's chosen people. Hopefully, the U.S. will have a political revolution (a bit of anarchy) and we will depart from our empire mentality, bring our troops home to protect our own borders and forget globalization. The Muslims will kill each other off, if left alone, remember T.E. Lawrence! And leave the rest of the world to its own demise, but if the USA is attacked or threatened, pull out all the stops and use the nukes!!

One of the problems we face involves race relations and immoral behavior, which included homosexual marriages and the promotion of a homosexual agenda. The idea that there are no differences between races and cultures is stupid. Of course there are innate differences as well as behavioral thinking. We should recognize and carefully examine these differences and work on ways to better understand an tolerate the factors and thinking that make us different so we can co-exist under equal protection of the law without any one race or culture receiving any special privileges granted by government. Regarding homosexuality, we must recognize that same sex intercourse in against the laws of nature, we have an innate sex drive to procreate and this is why sex is such a strong emotional desire. Two people of the same sex engaged in intercourse cannot reproduce anything – well, maybe a breeding ground for AIDS.

Why are elected officials and judges be so very tolerant of immoral and obscene behavior and so against the righteous and moral promotion of Godly displays and action? Well, I think I have answered this question. When a judge does take a moral stand he is forced into retirement, or dismissed. Remember Judge Moore? Judge Roy Moore was forced to resign his job as judge because he refused to remove the Ten Commandments from his court house; while, our courts insist in allowing Planned Parenthood promote teen-age abortions without notification or permission of parents. The fact that abortion is legal is insane. The "law" allows the killing or innocent unborn babies, but refuses to allow a Judge display the "Ten Commandments?"

We have a rule of law enforced by hypocrites. While the United States government condemned Saddam Hussein for "killing his own people, we allow abortionist to kill over 1.5 innocent unborn babies every year---- now, tell me again about genocide. Not to mention the number of our own people killed by the U.S. Government at Waco, Wounded Knee, Kent State, Ruby Ridge, and the Civil War. I guess it depends on who is doing the killing as to whether or not they are classified as atrocities --- and who is reporting the news.

At what point do the voters of this country stand up and demand that this staggering abuse of power and malfeasant servant of the people be removed? Will it ever happen? Or will continue to slide down a slippery slope to total enslavement. How dare this sack of putrescent horse dung demand an investigation of decent American political thought such as they have with many tax protestors and those who disagree with their unconstitutional laws. Who on earth do these corrupt, disgraceful lunatic think they are? Well, unfortunately, they know who they are, they are the empowered ones. "We The Sheeple" have allowed them to grab control of our lives, our freedoms and our children's future. I am sorry that I did not chose politics as a career, at an early age in life. Had I known that people like Obama, Bush, John McCain, and the likes of Nancy Polosi, and Harry Reed would be making decisions for our nation, I would have entered politics or maybe, left the country.

Polosi is a piece of work, or a piece of "corrupted degenerate"; take your pick. She is a disgrace to our nation; a disgrace to the House of Representatives; and a threat to human decency and moral values. This foolish "witch" is a selfish narcissist and a prime example of a treasonous political hack, declaring war on the people of our once great country and attempting to criminalize opposing political opinions. She is dangerous to freedom.

This abuse of power should not be tolerated, even if the people need to rise up against her and other tyrants in a bloody revolution (my opinion – First Amendment Right).

With the talking heads of TV; such as, Beck, O'Rielly, Matthews, Brown; Gretta, etc.; etc., I understand why we stay confused, and I do not believe it is by accident.

The best example I know is Glenn Beck's phony history lessons regarding civil rights, If Beck knew anything about truth in government and the movement against segregation, he would understand that the word "civil" designates "government," and government cannot guarantee rights. "Rights" come from God, Government can only grant privileges. It's because of the confusion between rights and privileges that our nation has so many problems. Ask any American in today's society if everyone should have the right to a free education and 99% will say, "Yes." You must go back and read the tenth plank in "The Ten Planks of Communism." Education is privilege, not a right. One of the worse decision ever made was to force our schools to integrate. Now, before you get you panties in a wad, let me say that no one should be denied the privilege to go to school, regardless of race or religion, but it is not "a right." When forced integration was introduced into our educational system, standards were compromised, as well as discipline. Children were bussed across towns and quotas were set, and the educational system digressed, and standards compromised. We went from a system that was concerned about students running in the halls, and breaking in the lunch room line, to a system concerned with drugs, violence, teen pregnancy, and birth control, and it all started about 1954 (Brown v. The Board of Education). Check the history and make an honest observation. No, I am not saying a person should be denied an education or the privilege of an education, as long as they can meet the standards and fit into a structured system, well discipline, and follow rules; no busing, no quotas, and no special consideration for lack of intelligence, then the privilege should not be denied. The idea of trade schools and/or vocational schools was needed then and is needed now, to accommodate those students, who cannot adjust in a structured and well disciplined educational environment. Also, bring back the reform schools for those students who refuse to adjust and obey the rule of law; and cause problems in the class room. It is hard to admit to the truth, is it not?

Beck's assessment of the civil rights movement is distorted. He has it all wrong. The Civil rights Act was responsible for placing many blacks in the position of becoming public parasites, and created agencies which promote corrupt politicians, lazy people, and criminals. Had our Constitution been properly interpreted and the law equally applied, there would have been no justification for Civil Rights legislation. Blacks have been exploited and propagandized to believe that a vote for a certain individual, such as Obama, and others before him would provide special privileges for them, which has not been true. Regardless of what the government does, we must recognize that there will always be hate, and distrust between races, religions, cultures, and ethnic groups. The only way to remove unwanted fears, hate, and distrust is through the teachings of Christ, and a respect for "Common Law." There is nothing wrong with integration or segregation as long it is "freedom of choice," and not forced upon people by the government. Each person should have the privilege of choosing his or her associates, and friends. It when people such as the late George Wallace, Lester Maddox, and the KKK use race to divide people, and promote hate for political gain or power, that we become suspicious of members of another race, and lose focus on the corruption and immoral practice of politicians, bureaucrats and phony leadership and develop a sense of hate because of color. Jesse Jackson and Al Sharpton continues to "stir the racial pot," promoting the hate of whites among blacks. These hypocrites do not want peace between the races, as it would diminish their income and base of power. As long as they can persuade blacks that white want to keep them as second class citizens and convince blacks that they are "subjects" in a white man's world, the mistrust and division will continue.

The media and the entertainment business shares in the roll of bringing down moral values in America, which has corrupted our system, and dumb down our educational system... I know that I am redundant in asking this question, but here goes anyway, "Do you remember the day when profanity and obscenities were not used in the entertainment business?" I can remember the day when or if someone used God's name in vain, they were shunned; pre-marital sex was considered a sin, and homosexuality was considered perverted.

If you want to know the names of the media and entertainment moguls, and mavens, who are responsible for the materials published, shown, and/ or spoken, please request a copy of my notes and research papers, which are free. You can make this request by simply sending me an email at braunkenh@aol.com.

You should be convinced that the talking heads on television and on the radio are only promoting the agenda of their "bosses." Listen and watch with a skeptical eye and ears. Do not believe what you are told. Do your own research ---- "seek the truth!"

CHAPTER NINE: MY PERSONAL EXPERIENCE AND WHY I AM QUALIFIED TO WRITE THIS BOOK

For three years in the early nineties, I worked with lobbyist, in Washington, D.C. and Little Rock, Arkansas. Some were Democrats and one was a Republican. Wayne Bishop was the Republican. He had worked with Reagan and helped organize "Democrats for Reagan." The others were Democrats, since Bill Clinton was President, we needed Democrats to achieve our objectives, which was to get sanctions removed by the United States and the UN form Libya, and Iraq; also, to help establish the infrastructure for Palestine. I just happened into this situation because of a Greek; Spyro Armennis was dating a cousin of a person with whom I knew in the oil and gas drilling business in Kentucky. Spyro came to me seeking funding for a drilling program in Kentucky using banks guarantees from Arabic banks.

My connection was David Howe, who was then a Senior Vice President at NationsBank in Nashville, Tennessee. David was a member of the Nashville Committee on Foreign Relations and later assisted me in becoming a member. David had a personal relationship with the Howard Baker law firm, which Lamar Alexander was a partner, and Lawrence Eagleburger was a public relations specialist. This was the kind of influence needed by rouge nations. I first approached David about a loan with the guarantees from an Arabic bank, but when Spyro told me about Libya, I quickly change my direction and wanted to pursue the political challenge of getting sanctions lifted. The fist mention of sanction involved Libya only, Iraq and Palestine came later. Spyro had developed a relationship in Greece with George Hallaq. Hallaq was a Palestinian, who father was a Bishop in the Greek Orthodox Church, until his death. Hallaq was also an adviser to Andres Papandreou, former Greek Prime Minister, now deceased. Hallaq had all the contacts needed in the Middle East to make the introductions.

So, after Spyro and I convinced the Baker firm that we seemed legitimate, they implied they would take the challenge with us. Looking back, I do not think they believed us, at the time, and were only testing us to see if we really had the contacts to get Libya as clients.

Not long after that meeting, Dave Howe and I met Spyro in Fairfield, Connecticut, and from there to Newark airport, headed for Tunis, Tunisia. There were several of us traveling together, included in the trip was Spyro, David Howe, John Williams (cousin worked for ABC news), Rita Rankin (Al Gore's former girlfriend), Donna Thrower, a friend of Rita's and Spyro "sleep-in girl friend," and me.

We were net Tunis by an entourage of Libyan and Tunisian officials who took us through customs quickly and privately. We were transported to the Tunis Hilton Hotel. There I met George Hallaq for the first time. He introduced me to Daniel Ortega, from Nicaragua, and leader of the Sandinistas. He and his family had been invited to meet with the same officials we were to meet in Libya and later in Iraq.

We arrived the next day in Libya, and two days later met with officials, and eventually met with Qathafi (sometimes spelled "Quaddafi and sometime with a "G"). Our mission was to write a plan to get sanctions against Libya removes, and find a way to get it implemented, which also entailed a plan to solve the Pan Am 103 bombing problem. Libya was accused of being responsible for downing Pan Am 103 over Lockerbie, Scotland. I was assigned to the task of writing the plan, including its implementation, which I did and the plan was used, but I was never paid the millions of dollars promised. I do not think Qathafi was ever told that I was "stiffed," by his hirelings, including Obedi, his official assigned to the case, alomng with Ayad Tayari, Libya's ambassador to Greece, and my contact. I still have my files, well secured. I made the mistake of meeting and revealing my plan to Alan Gerson, attorney for some of the family members killed on the Pan Am flight, I believe he took the plan I presented to him and use it to settle the case. Billions were paid by Libya to get the case settled and sanctions lifted, for a crime, which, in my opinion, they did not commit.

The lobbyist I worked with were paid though me with cash of $98,000 and $500 thousand bearer notes, which I "hammered" in Switzerland (UBS), and in the Isle of Man (Bank of Ireland), using a Greek shipping company for justification of payment for services.

Getting back to my story, after meeting in Libya, we returned to Tunis. Later, we went to Jordan, where we had breakfast in King Hessians Palace, and I met Arafat for the first time. Officials from Iraq were at the breakfast meeting, and arrangements were made for us to enter Iraq. Remember, we could not travel on a U.S. Passport, as the State Department had restricted travel to both Libya and Iraq. We traveled on a special visa issued by each government. I visited Baghdad twice, and money was paid to Joe Purvis, an attorney, lobbyist in Little Rock, to help remove sanctions on Iraq for medical and humane purposes. Joe never delivered and kept the money

I can truthfully say, the war in Iraq was staged, and Libya was set up. Palestine and its people are victims of a ruthless Israeli government. I may be doing another book on this subject; so, I will end this part of my story here by stating that meeting many people in D.C.; Little Rock; Europe, and the Middle East forced me to do an incremental amount of research and reading. Based on what I learned and observed, I believe little of what government official say, and less coming from the media. I know the truth!

My experience with Arafat and his wife Suha was one which I shall never forget. One meeting was in their home in Tunis. Arafat arrived shortly after Spyro and I had lunch. Suha had remembered that I was vegetarian, and had the chefs prepare a vegetarian meal for me. Arafat had just completed and signed the Oslo Peace Accord with Rabin, Prime Minister of Israel, and was very excited about Palestine becoming a separate State. Unfortunately, Rabin was assassinated. The assassination of Yitzhak Rabin was an attack on the peace process, and an attack on peace loving Jews; the Zionist then took control. The conflict is about real-estate and racism, among other things. These are the same Zionist who controls the Jewish lobbyist in the U.S. You will also find them in key financial positions, and in control of the media. Nevertheless, they are extremely smart, and if they could be converted to Christianity could lead the world to permanent prosperity and a control of the world's population growth by moral means, rather than war, abortion, starvation, disease, etc., etc. The average IQ of Jews is about 15 pts higher than Caucasians, and about 25 pts higher than blacks (See: Bell Curve).

I know Jews have an innate ability to reason, especially, when it comes to financial matters, and negotiations. Jews are creative and have the tenacity to survive under adverse conditions. Even though I am against the Zionism, my heart is with Israel and it survival at any price; even if it includes siding with Zionist…. As stated earlier, my Grandfather was a Jew!

CHAPTER TEN: COMMENTS, EMAILS, AND RANDOM INFROMATION

This Chapter is dedicated to friends and others who have emailed me information regarding, our government, the economy, and international politics. I want the reader to realize that there are about 20 million Americans who are aware of the problems our once great nation face, we are in a struggle for freedoms, and the future looks bleak.

Remember the adage *"The enemy of my enemy is my friend"*. This accurately sums up the gruesome marriage of the power hungry "Left" to wannabe world dominating Islam followers, both at the manipulative behest of our insatiably greedy "international financial oligarchy". Both the destructive Left and Islamic ignorance hold hands in virulently detesting freedom and hating anything and everything associated with it. The Left generously does not promise to brutally murder you over a difference of opinion by grotesquely decapitating you with a rusty scimitar; Islam does. Islam is a pseudo-religion that outlived its usefulness to civilization several bloody centuries ago.

The Left on the other hand will simply starve you to death and blame the "Czars or Bush." The Leftist track record so loved by Hollywood confirms hundreds of millions starved, tortured, imprisoned and murdered by their empathetic heroes, Lenin, Mao, Castro, Pol Pot, etc. They proudly sport colorful t-shirts with pictures of butcher Ernesto "Che" Guevara. Our favorite journalism morons and pundits can be counted on either to lie or opine stupidly depending on their indoctrinating alma mater. We have become pathetic comic book, caricatures of our past, cowering timidly beneath political correctness; afraid to speak or even acknowledge the simple and obvious truth. If this remains our willing choice; we cannot possibly remain free. Freedom requires courage, truth, honor and dignity. The Left and its new foot soldier Islam offer none of these.

How about a biblical adage, say Matthew 7:20? *"You can tell a tree by its fruit"*. What does it matter whether Obama, a known liar, incapable of shutting his mouth for even ten minutes, claims to be Christian or Muslim? Obama couldn't find the truth if he tripped on it. High crimes and misdemeanors champion, Barack Hussein Obama is a well publicized, demonstrative, not to mention proud, Islamic supporter. He publically bows to Islamic leaders. His destructive policies, both domestic and foreign, reek of U.S. hatred specifically and drip with malevolence toward liberty generally. He has dishonored our country and Judeo-Christian heritage, insulted every friend and embraced every enemy of human dignity, yet fully half the country thinks he's doing a good job. Doesn't say much for American education or survival instinct does it? Says even less about ignorant, gutter journalism.

Our American celebration of loss has become so pandemic I can't help but wonder if it's a Bilderberg Steering Committee strategy dreamed up by David Rockefeller, Vernon Jordan, Paul Wolfowitz, Henry Kissinger or some other traitorous, Logan Act violating, slime to condition Americans to value loosing. There was a time when America and her allies celebrated victory and life. Today our supposed leaders assure there is no victory, despise life and apparently are conditioning us to celebrate loss. How motivational. How uplifting. How patriotic.

In America today we openly and enthusiastically celebrate and construct death monuments to victim hood and murder. We do it in Washington D.C., Manhattan, Oklahoma City, New Orleans and God knows where else. I'm sorry, but this is sick. **We appropriately mourn murder, not celebrate it.** Islam and the Left celebrate death as a victory dance and a vibrant path to power and domination. For any civilization to adopt such backward, self mutilating thinking is a sign certain of coming extinction. The will to live and to love has apparently been extinguished.

We foolishly elected a President and Congress that by intent or ignorance, but certainly by action, hate our country, our people and our friends. For God's sake, do we have to hate ourselves as well? **Know them by their fruit.** Vote knowledgeably. Pay attention.

Bruce J. Kolinski, P.E.

The next email is from a retired person, with grandchildren, who is very concern with the direction our nation is heading.

	Ann & Bill Bolling View Contact	
To:	Undisclosed-Recipient@yahoo.com	

This Is Why There Are No Jobs in America.

By Porter Stansberry
Saturday, August 21, 2010
I'd like to make you a business offer. Seriously, this is a real offer. In fact, you really can't turn me down, as you'll come to understand in a moment...

Here's the deal. You're going to start a business or expand the one you've got now. It doesn't really matter what you do or what you're going to do. I'll partner with you no matter what business you're in – as long as it's legal.

But I can't give you any capital – you have to come up with that on your own. I won't give you any labor – that's definitely up to you. What I will do, however, is demand you follow all sorts of rules about what products and services you can offer, how much (and how often) you pay your employees, and where and when you're allowed to operate your business. That's my role in the affair: to tell you what to do.

Now in return for my rules, I'm going to take roughly half of whatever you make in the business each year. Half seems fair, doesn't it? I think so. Of course, that's half of your profits.

You're also going to have to pay me about 12% of whatever you decide to pay your employees because you've got to cover my expenses for promulgating all of the rules about who you can employ, when, where, and how. Come on, you're my partner. It's only "fair."

Now... after you've put your hard-earned savings at risk to start this business, and after you've worked hard at it for a few decades (paying me my 50% or a bit more along the way each year), you might decide you'd like to cash out – to finally live the good life.

Whether or not this is "fair" – some people never can afford to retire – is a different argument. As your partner, I'm happy for you to sell whenever you'd like... because our agreement says, if you sell, you have to pay me an additional 20% of whatever the capitalized value of the business is at that time.

I know... I know... you put up all the original capital. You took all the risks. You put in all of the labor. That's all true. But I've done my part, too. I've collected 50% of the profits each year. And I've always come up with more rules for you to follow each year. Therefore, I deserve another, final 20% slice of the business.

Oh... and one more thing...

Even after you've sold the business and paid all of my fees... I'd recommend buying lots of life insurance. You see, even after you've been retired for years, when you die, you'll have to pay me 50% of whatever your estate is worth.

After all, I've got lots of partners and not all of them are as successful as you and your family. We don't think its "fair" for your kids to have such a big advantage. But if you buy enough life insurance, you can finance this expense for your children.

All in all, if you're a very successful entrepreneur... if you're one of the rare, lucky, and hard-working people who can create a new company, employ lots of people, and satisfy the public... you'll end up paying me more than 75% of your income over your life. Thanks so much.

I'm sure you'll think my offer is reasonable and happily partner with me... but it doesn't really matter how you feel about it because if you ever try to stiff me – or cheat me on any of my fees or rules – I'll break down your door in the middle of the night, threaten you and your family with heavy, automatic weapons, and throw you in jail.

That's how civil society is supposed to work, right? This is Amerika, isn't it?

That's the offer Amerika gives its entrepreneurs. And the idiots in Washington wonder why there are no new jobs...

The next email was sent to me from Johnny Omohundro, a Doctor, who studies politics and economics.

From: <rolnthundr@ > (go to this webpage)

Subject: Fwd: EXTERNAL: Overwhelm the System

Date: Saturday, August 21, 2010, 5:30 PM

Food for thought! **REMEMBER IN NOVEMBER!** - Just a little incentive to show up at the polls....every time!

More significant evidence to throw out the incumbents in November 2010! In

Case you haven't figured out what's happening, here's a wrap-up of the program.

"Overwhelm the System,"
By **Wayne Allyn Root**

Barrack Obama is no fool. He is not incompetent. To the contrary, he is brilliant. He knows exactly what he's doing. He is purposely overwhelming the U.S. economy to create systemic failure, economic crisis and social chaos --thereby destroying capitalism and our country from within.

Barack Obama is my college classmate (Columbia University, class of '83). As Glenn Beck correctly predicted from day one, Obama is following the plan of Cloward and Piven, two professors at Columbia University. They outlined a plan to socialize America by overwhelming the system with government spending and entitlement demands. Add up the clues below. Taken individually they're alarming. Taken as a whole, it is a brilliant, Machiavellian game plan to turn the United States into a socialist/Marxist state with a permanent majority that desperately needs government for survival ... and can be counted on to always vote for bigger government. Why not? They have no responsibility to pay for it.

Universal health care. The health care bill had very little to do with health care. Â It had everything to do with unionizing millions of hospital and health care workers, as well as adding 15,000 to 20,000 new IRS agents (who will join government employee unions). Obama doesn't care that giving free health care to 30 million Americans will add trillions to the national debt. What he does care about is that it cements the dependence of those 30 million voters to Democrats and big government. Who but a socialist revolutionary would pass this reckless spending bill in the middle of a depression?

Cap and trade. Like health care legislation having nothing to do with health care, cap and trade has nothing to do with global warming. It has everything to do with redistribution of income, government control of the economy and a criminal payoff to Obama's biggest contributors. Those powerful and wealthy unions and contributors (like GE, which owns NBC, MSNBC and CNBC) can then be counted on to support everything Obama wants. They will kickback hundreds of millions of dollars in contributions to Obama and the Democratic Party to keep them in power. The bonus is that all the new taxes on Americans with bigger cars, bigger homes and businesses help Obama "spread the wealth around."

Make Puerto Rico a state. Why? Who's asking for a 51st state? Who's asking for millions of new welfare recipients and government entitlement addicts in the middle of a depression? Certainly not American taxpayers. But this has been Obama's plan all along. His goal is to add two new Democrat senators, five Democrat congressman and a million loyal Democratic voters who are dependent on big government.

Legalize 12 million illegal immigrants. Just giving these 12 million potential new citizens free health care alone could overwhelm the system and bankrupt America. But it adds 12 million reliable new Democrat voters who can be counted on to support big government. Add another few trillion dollars in welfare, aid to dependent children, food stamps, free medical, education, tax credits for the poor, and eventually Social Security.

Stimulus and bailouts. Where did all that money go? It went to Democrat contributors, organizations (ACORN), and unions -- including billions of dollars to save or create jobs of government employees across the country. It went to save GM and Chrysler so that their employees could keep paying union dues. It went to AIG so that Goldman Sachs could be bailed out (after giving Obama almost $1 million in contributions). A staggering $125 billion went to teachers (thereby protecting their union dues). All those public employees will vote loyally Democrat to protect their bloated salaries and pensions that are bankrupting America. The country goes broke, future generations face a bleak future, but Obama, the Democrat Party, government, and the unions grow more powerful. The ends justify the means.

<u>Raise taxes on small business owners, high-income earners, and job creators</u>.

Put the entire burden on only the top 20 percent of taxpayers, redistribute the income, punish success, and reward those who did nothing to deserve it (except vote for Obama). Reagan wanted to dramatically cut taxes in order to starve the government. Obama wants to dramatically raise taxes to starve his political opposition. – End

With the acts outlined above, Obama and his regime have created a vast and rapidly expanding constituency of voters dependent on big government; a vast privileged class of public employees who work for big government; and a government dedicated to destroying capitalism and installing themselves as socialist rulers by overwhelming the system.

Add it up and you've got the perfect Marxist scheme -- all devised by my Columbia University college classmate Barack Obama using the Cloward and Piven Plan.

There are people that will simply read and ignore this... maybe not read it at all. There are others that are so wrapped up with Obama-mania that they will never accept any criticism of him. There are those that say, 'I'm too old to worry about this crap... it's not going to affect me'!

Finally, there are professional blood-suckers that live off everyone else's sweat -- they want more 'Free Stuff'. And we all know where they stand. If you care about your future, or maybe your children or grandchildren's future, do something now.

<u>Vote the bums out of office this November</u>. And, make Obama a one-term President.

"The Congress....Desirous...to have people of all ranks and degrees duly impressed with a solemn sense of God's superintending providence, and of their duty, devoutly to rely...on His aid and direction...Do earnestly recommend Friday, the 17th day of May be observed by the colonies as a day of humiliation, fasting, and prayer; that we may, with united hearts, confess and bewailed our

manifold sins and transgressions, and, by sincere repentance and amendment of life, appease God's righteous displeasure, and, through the merits and mediation of Jesus Christ, obtain this pardon and forgiveness."

— The Continental Congress, May 16, 1776 --- END----

As you can see, others are just as concern as I, but we need more people to get involved and do everything in their power to turn the United States around and get back to Constitutional law.

The next email is very interesting.

08-22-2010: World War III

thekolinskichronicle | August 22, 2010 at 8:58 am | Tags: Abbas, Iran, Middle East, Netanyahu, oil, Palestine, World War III | Categories: The Progressive Papers | URL: http://wp.me/pC2Ts-iA

Final arrangements are now being made for the grand opening of World War III. The schedule hasn't been locked in, but the plot has been written, the theater has been hired, the props are being constructed, the players have been invited to the stage and are busy choosing sides, though they likely don't realize the sides were determined long ago. The sides don't matter much anyway. The name of the game is WIN OR LOSE. What matters is the war itself, the money to be made and the One World, political power shift that will inevitably result regardless the apparent winner. In terms of freedom and individual liberty, all winners in this war are losers, just as in WW I and WW II. The insanely greedy, world financial oligarchy is sipping fine wine, cognac and doing its director thing; the major world populations have been thoroughly conditioned and propagandized, have read for their parts and are all now salivating for a part, any bit part in this grand tragedy, the "Mother of All Plays".

Unfortunately, this isn't a dress rehearsal, nor a play; its real life and we're all in it for real. I suspect, as citizens and voters, in the U.S. at least, we should have paid more attention to the motivations and positions of our supposed political representatives. Freedom is a serious task master and we have wandered seriously off task. Our country is now led by insipid morons and corrupt, cowardly, self aggrandizing losers. The world population has now trapped itself as players to the death on planet earth, just as the unwilling students of Koushun Takami's novel, Battle Royale were trapped on the island of Kyushu to play out their grisly battle for survival. How will it turn out? Must it happen? Can it be avoided? If "we the people" don't wake from our political coma soon and get off this bus, it is guaranteed to turn out badly and will inevitably become a self fulfilling prophesy. The oligarchies are masters of the inevitable. Just has the students of Battle Royale were drugged while on their bus and were transported to an unknown destiny, "we the people" have been asleep and are finding it difficult and challenging to regain consciousness. We continue to sleep at our family's peril.

WW III is intended to accomplish a number of things that the oligarchic families would like to see. First of all, there's always good money for the oligarchy in financing both sides and all sides of any war. Lord knows how many staggeringly, beautiful yachts have been paid for and sail regularly, powered with this blood soaked money. Secondly, the earth's population will be significantly reduced. The oligarchy families don't like the little people wasting resources that can better be utilized by the oligarchy for their own future purposes. It is the oligarchy's judgment that there are far too many little people on earth to be useful. It does not require 100 little people to polish a Bentley, nor to cook a soufflé. Dead little people potentially make good fertilizer and in any case, no longer waste precious non-renewable resources.

I don't pretend to have any idea what the intended schedule for the grand opening of WW III is; I'm just an over the road truck driver with too much time to think on his hands. Most likely there will be an opening act or two before the grand finale. For example, Israel has just been cast for the lead role as protagonist in the first act. Iran is the antagonist. Benjamin Netanyahu is a very smart, very tough guy. He has always staunchly stood against Israel giving up any of its postage stamp size land. Such compromise in the past has simply and conveniently relocated the Islamic rocket launch sites for thousands of rockets closer to major Israeli population centers; and bolstered the 1985 intifada, resulting in untold misery, mutilation, death and sorrow for both Israelis and Palestinians.

Yet, suddenly Netanyahu is generously and cooperatively volunteering compromise and talks with Palestinian Authority President Mahmud Abbas. What? Why is this happening on the birthing eve of Iranian nuclear power? I suspect the average Palestinian would prefer a real life to continuous slaughter, but Palestinian leadership has been historically obsessed with the wholesale destruction of Israel at any cost. You may as well discuss opportunity with a stump as with Palestinian leaders. Maybe Abbas has had a change of heart? Who knows, but I doubt it? These silly talks are a great photo op for both Hillary and Barack, who will likely be incompetently all over it; all over the New York Times that is. Neither of them can stand face to face with Benjamin Netenyahu and remain on their feet, looking him in the eye for even a minute. Won't happen. The U.SA. Will gain nothing from these talks except photo op time for both Barack and Hillary prior to the November elections.

What does Netenyahu have to gain? This is obvious. Former U.S. Ambassador to the United Nations, John Bolton told us last week that these talks have nothing to do with Iran. Bolton usually has it right, but why would he say something so naive? Did he adopt this strange position as a result of this year's Bilderberg meeting? Just kidding. Clearly Netanyahu has no choice, but to attack Iran before Iran gains nuclear weapons. The entire world has timidly backed off even discussing the insane Iranian leadership in realistic terms. The President of the United States can hardly be identified as anything less than an animated Islamic cheer leader. This leaves Israel with having to defend itself and be the GO-TO country. Given the limited choices available, Netanyahu is making the only play left open. He is garnering all the geopolitical capital and good will he can prior to attacking Iran. Next week's White House talks are a throw away negotiation as Palestinian leadership will never agree to anything short of Israel's destruction anyway. Netanyahu understands this more clearly than anyone and must do what he has to do.

This well orchestrated Iranian disaster is just the opening act and we don't know how quickly it may escalate; but short of a miracle, it surely will. Russia, China, Korea and Pakistan are already lined up behind Iran. Europe and Japan, for their own protection will line up behind the U.S. Australia and Canada will do what Australia and Canada always do; and they won't be on the side of Islamic jihad. India will be left with no options, the same as Israel. The lines in the sand are already drawn. If we don't wake up soon, the predominant color in the world will be red and much of it will be our own.

One possible miracle would be for the average American voter, whether Democrat, Republican, Libertarian or Independent to realize that our elected and appointed Federal government has sold us down the oligarchy's creek without a paddle. Why should anyone in the U.S., or Europe for that matter give two hoots what goes on in the Middle East? The Middle East sand box has no importance or significance in the world other than that which has been artificially orchestrated and created. The created importance is, of course, oil for oil driven world economy. The oligarchy has conditioned our government(s) to ignore and even fight or damage our own independent oil sources thereby creating a significant worldwide dependence on the Middle East. Russian and American oil resources alone dwarf Middle East oil reserves, yet we are blindly conditioned to remain dependent upon an Islamic culture and ideology that detests us as infidels and dreams of world domination. We are all pawns in this very real game.

The good people of the Middle East are being used and manipulated just as the West is. If you think about this, it's pretty stupid for either Russia, America, Europe or the Middle East people to buy into this hateful nonsense; but we all have and in doing so have constructed a Middle East dependency which has now become the sensitive, hair trigger for World War III. Israel as the main mark, is forced to pull the trigger and then this nuclear war - and it will be nuclear - will bring the world's thoroughly conned population, particularly the American middle class to its bloody knees, so that once and for all the oligarchy will finally have re-established worldwide feudalism under their control.

Obviously I have come to believe that the American and European political systems are badly broken and are now easily manipulated to their own misfortune by the world's financial oligarchy for its own greedy ends. This is a sad situation with a possible tragic ending, but it can easily be fixed for the entire world by individual American citizens standing up and proclaiming "ENOUGH IS ENOUGH". If the little people will stand together the oligarchy is stopped in its bloodthirsty, immoral tracks. There is nothing the oligarchy can do if "WE" say "NO": if America refuses to play the game or to enter onto the stage; its game over; curtain down. As citizen's we have this power. The question is do we have the courage and good sense to use it?

The U.S. Constitutional Republic based on the unalienable rights and human dignity granted by virtue of our Creation, by our Creator and as enumerated by our Founders is the salvation of our freedom and the preservation of freedom for the rest of the world. WE each have a moral responsibility to stand up to this task; or not. Not to choose is to choose. I hope for the sake of our world's children we all wake up and choose.

This next email was from Bruce also, we have discussed the issues include in his email several times, but he seems to have summed it up nicely:

The reason most of our U.S. Senators and House Members no longer represent their voting constituents is "career politics" in union with the 17th Amendment. The obvious fix is term limits on the one hand and if possible, repeal of the horrendously disastrous 17th Amendment.

If you've ever attempted any sort of mechanical or handy-man work you've likely encountered the "stripped screw" conundrum. As you attempt to tighten the screw securely, the threads begin to shear (strip) and before you know it; you can't tighten the screw any further and most likely may also have difficulty removing it so it can be replaced with a sound screw. In the process of trying to do all this, you've probably managed to further damage whatever it was you were trying to fix. A career politician is exactly like one of these bargain basement screws. Once you get them in, they won't do the job and even worse, because of Gerrymandering, now you can't get them out. The system has effectively been stripped and is no longer secure.

This criticism doesn't suggest politicians are necessarily bad people. It just recognizes that human nature is what it is and the effective management of humans requires acknowledgment of human strengths and weaknesses. Any situational context promoting success is much better from a constructive behavior standpoint than a context maximizing the probability of failure. Fortunately for us as Americans, our Founders were well aware of our human tendencies and created a healthy, balanced, self checking context – our Constitutional Republic – for us to function within.

Unfortunately, Communists, having an indoctrinated animus toward individual liberty, have inserted themselves into our political process and through such deceitful mechanisms as the 17th Amendment, successfully undone the self checking mechanism between our House and the Senate, thereby intentionally unbalancing the system. The system is now stripped, so to speak, is more easily manipulated by political operatives and no longer works effectively for "we the people". The Communist / socialist / progressive / liberal / leftist thrust is always toward freedom strangling "centralized government control", the ultimate result of which is government tyranny either by totalitarian dictate or by Royal mandate. In either case "we the people" are reduced to loyal serfs or as I might more coarsely phrase it, slaves.

Community organizers, always feeding at some part of the "greasy public trough" are never held responsible for the success of any outcome. They carefully stay away from real work having real accountability standards for performance. This cowardly, irresponsible and vacuous existence allows them to grow up as indoctrinated, arrogant fools who vainly believe all societal ills are some sort of academic exercise. Since everything they have in life is given to them by their leftist handlers in exchange for their minds and souls, they learn to live outside of daily reality as non-functional intellectual snobs who never tire of hearing themselves speak. The communist organizer stands intellectually, emotionally and dishonestly separate from the repeated historic and current failure of his or her collectivist doctrine. Heavily protected within their secure cocoon of "public taking" they are isolated from the harsh nature of economic survival on the streets of life. This protected parasitical life style within life's normal painful reality is what permits the organizer to irrationally ignore consistent failure, mindlessly treating the brutal dehumanizing results of their doctrine as some sort of detached academic exercise. More than one hundred million starved; raped, tortured, imprisoned and murdered across the globe at the hands of leftists is not an academic exercise.

Stealing more than a trillion honest tax payer dollars within 18 months and gifting it to politically correct friends and allies, thereby draining the private sector of job creating capital is not an academic exercise. There is nothing academic about losing your family business or your job; having your family car repossessed; losing your family home; or being unable to feed and clothe your children. The embarrassment and financial pain of a father or mother destroying 40 years of excellent, hard earned credit over a one year failed period because your career politicians are playing politics with our nation's money supply is not academic. The BP oil spill is not an academic exercise. A nuclear Iran allied with Russia and/or Communist China is not an academic exercise. The U.S. betrayal of the people of Israel is not an academic exercise. Expanding the Afghan war into Pakistan, with a Muslim population of 140,000,000 is not an academic exercise. Destroying the world's finest health care system is not an academic exercise. Expanding our national debt to 4 times the already criminal level of malfeasance displayed by the Bush Administration is not an academic exercise.

If we wish to be free of the rapidly expanding cage of unconstitutional, illegal and unjust Federal government control and corruption a good start would be to impose term limits on Members of the Senate and House of Representatives. Two terms is it. Today's elected representative is gifted with a salary four times the national average, full pension after a single term and health benefits that would embarrass a pick pocket, not to mention the golden key – a license to steal – the people's wealth. Congressional redistricting (gerrymandering) enables near perpetual re-election. Human nature must be reigned in and politicians are no exception. Elected representatives should receive a salary set at the national average. They should be required to purchase their own health insurance just as any business owner is. They should receive no pension what-so-ever. Serving your country should be an honor and a sacrifice, not a license to live lavishly, at tax payer expense and to abuse the hard earned wealth of our country's citizens.

Secondly, repeal the 17th Amendment. U.S. Senators are intended to be appointed by the various elected State legislatures. This removes Senators from the political mud wrestling arena, where money and influence reign supreme. Senators appointed by their State of residency will represent the best interests of their respective State or they will lose their appointment. Publicly elected Senators as made possible by the Communist inspired 17th Amendment have reduced the U.S. Senate to a collection of money pandering con-artists subject to the vagaries of financial corruption and media manipulation. The Senatorial check on Congressional power put in place by our Founders has been eliminated. This has functionally reduced the U.S. Senate to a box of stripped screws. They no longer have value to "we the people" and are in a position to do great harm. BY destroying the legislative balance between the House and Senate, Congress has effectively been marginalized, thereby defaulting tremendous ungoverned power to the Executive Branch. The 17th Amendment does not work and it is an important cog in the freedom eating wheel of socialist organizers. Individual liberty requires its repeal.

Personally, I'm tired of trying to work with a bunch of stripped screws peddled to us by the bargain basement flea markets at RNC and DNC. Let's appoint our Senators and get some new House Members; quality ones – "Drink some Tea." It can be good for you and for your family.

By: Bruce J. Kolinski, P.E.

"CONCLUSSION"

"A man, convinced against his will, is of the same opinion still!"

When I decided to write this book, I was a very apprehensive, as I knew that many of my close friends would find it offensive because I have disturbed their beliefs or exposed the truth of some icons, which they foolishly admire. Many so-called "conservatives," the majority of those reading this book, may simply sink into denial, and choose not believe anything that I have written, as my "truths" are too hard to "swallow and digest." Some people just can't handle the truth. I challenge anyone, however, including my friends, to disprove any written statement, presented as facts. You may disagree with my opinions, which this book is full of, but the factual evidence I have expressed cannot be disputed. If I am wrong in any facts presented herein, I will apologize and ask your forgiveness for misstating the truth. I, too, do not want to believe a lie.

While I did not dwell much on the Catholic Church, we do know that the Catholic Church and many priests have a corrupt past and committed ungodly acts, which are contrary to the teachings of the Bible. Hopefully, my Catholic friends will not be offended with my comment and will be open minded enough to seek the truth about the atrocities and misguided acts committed in the Church's past. I am not condemning my Catholic friends because all Christianity has fallen from Grace from time to time The Bible makes it simple when judging others (you judge based on actions and behavior). If a person, regardless of his/her church affiliation, accepts Christ as Savior and Lord; he/she will be save. Living for Christ is the only way for a Christian to prove their beliefs. One cannot live a sinful, deceitful, and degenerate life and have salvation, unless he repents, and accepts Jesus as Lord. More importantly, a person claiming to be a minister of God, cannot teach, or preach false doctrine and be saved. The "worse of the worse" are the hypocrites that use God for personal gains and for self serving interest, while claiming to ministers of God, preaching the Gospel.

Throughout this book, I have pointed out how the majority of the people are like sheep. This is why I entitle my book, "WE THE SHEEPLE" If you to examine the behavior of sheep, you will understand. Sheep have a natural instinct to follow the sheep in front of them. This is why slaughtering sheep is somewhat easy. When one sheep goes in a particular direction, the rest of the flock will usually follow, even if it is destructive. For example, if one sheep jumps over a cliff, the others are likely to follow. From the time they are born, lambs are conditioned to follow the older members of the flock. This is an innate characteristic of sheep. People are much the same. They are mostly followers and are always looking to someone else to take the lead in deciding their future and the laws they follow. Those of us, who are not "sheep," we usually find ourselves in some trouble with the authorities or looked upon as rebels, by the majority.

In Iceland there is a strain of sheep known as leader-sheep. Leader-sheep are highly intelligent animals that have the ability and instinct to lead a flock home during difficult conditions. We humans have "leader-sheep" among us. They are the ones who are the Elitist, and pass laws, control the currency, head up the international financial systems, control the media, and determine the domestic and foreign policies of nations. Of course, some of these "leader-sheep" turn into rebels, and lead the charge against those who want to deprive "the flock" of its freedoms. I am among the rebellious leader-sheep – it is a struggle!

The scientific study of animal behavior is called **Ethology**. The study of human behavior is called organizational psychology; or at least it is the best "scientific name" I could come up with to define "the study of human behavior;" Organizational behavior is an academic discipline concerned with describing, understanding, predicting, and controlling human behavior in an organizational environment. Psychology is also a term frequently used to define the study of human behavior, but the term alone does cover the complete study of human behavior in a structured environment. Since humans are members of the "animal kingdom," we have something in common with other animals. When selecting a title for this book, I thought a long time about which animal we have been compared to the most. I wanted an animal that would best illustrate our behavior, and after studying the behavior of sheep, I decided on the title, "We the Sheeple," referring to people as "sheeple". Throughout the Bible, people are compared to sheep (sheep are mentioned more than 500 times in the Bible). Even in our conversations, we sometimes refer to each other as looking sheepish; and calling rouge members of our families, "the black sheep of the family."

Sheep are a prey animal. When they are faced with danger, their natural instinct is to flee, not fight. Their strategy is to use avoidance and rapid flight to avoid being eaten. After fleeing, sheep will reform their group and look at the predator. They use their natural herding instinct to band together for safety. A sheep that is by itself is vulnerable to attack. They stay in herds and are often referred to as a "flock of sheep." Humans are both hunters and prey. We too have a need to stay together in a "flock" (tribes, communities, neighborhoods, societies, clubs, platoon, etc., etc.); as most believe there is safety in numbers.

Normally, like sheep, humans, when faced with a predator, instinctively will run. Most people will try to avoid confrontation and are very social minded, preferring to remain in a group as opposed to being isolated.

The enemies of sheep are carnivores that include herbivores in their diet. In the world of humans, the diet is both vegetarian and carnivores; most humans eat both meat and vegetables (including fruits). What we find in the human race are "political and economic carnivores." They prey upon the "Sheeple." These are the "vultures" of our societies; and they attack the most vulnerable, using the political and economic power they possess to devour our freedoms and wealth: thus, "We the Sheeple" has been written!

Tea Party Movement
I want to mention the "Tea Party Movement" again, and Sarah Palin. I would be remiss, if I did not point out how dangerous a movement for freedom is when it is captured by the establishment's puppets. I do not know if Palin is a member of any "Elitist organization," but I am suspicious of anyone who claims to be a conservative, but will defend those Neo Cons who claim to represent the conservative movement and are nothing more than hypocrites, such as Newt Gingrich, Sean Hannity, John McCain,

and the likes. I know that many of you still will not believe that Ronald Reagan was a liberal, even though I have given you his voting record; however, I leave it up to you to do your own research and determine the truth for yourself.

Just a few more words, regarding FOX and pseudo-conservatives:

There are many who will continue to believe that Bill O'Reilly is fair and balanced, and swallow his propaganda "hook, line, and sinker." I know that many of you will not accept the truth, even if all the facts are there for you to discover for yourself. Let me remind you that "Mr. Fair and Balanced (O'Reilly)" advocated war with Iraq stating that we had proof Saddam was hiding "weapons of mass destruction." Remember? Now, that the facts are known, which shows this to be a lie. O'Reilly simply dismisses all his touting for a war as a mistake and offers an apology. My question to O'Reilly is, "If I knew that the claim concerning Iraq's having WMD was a lie, and I am not in the media, nor do I have your news gathering resources, why did you not know?" Now, O'Reilly claims that he has proof that Obama was born in Hawaii. He has stated time and time again that he has seen copies of two newspapers from 1961 announcing Obama's birth. My questions is how simple would it be for some government agency or "insiders" to fabricate newspapers showing the proof that O'Reilly says he has seen, or to fabricate a fake birth certificate? Surely, "Mr. Fair and Balance" is not so naïve to think that this cannot be done. But for the sake of this conversation, let's say that Obama was born in Hawaii, in the United States, ***and I have no reason to believe otherwise***, except that the story will not go away; Frankly, I could care less, as where Obama was born could be anywhere the "government's puppeteers decide. If records could be "faked" to show WMD Iraq to start an "undeclared war," Obama's birth certificate would be rather easy to forge. I would like to know "who issued the passport Obama use when he was shuttling between New York, Jakarta, and Karachi?" Also, how could a young man, who arrived in New York in early June 1981, without the price of a hotel room in his pocket, suddenly come up with the price of a round-the-world trip just a month later? And once he was on a plane, shuttling between New York, Jakarta, and Karachi, what passport was he offering when he passed through Customs and Immigration. If truthfully answered, this should end the discussion and all doubt, and all the naysayers should shut-up, but, Mr. O'Reilly, please finish your investigation, and make sure that phony documents are not what you see. "Mr. Fair and Balance," let's discuss the subject of the First Amendment and the "Baptist Church rally/ protest" at a military funeral that members of the church used to protest the unconstitutional War in Iraq and Afghanistan…. O'Reilly does not like the message, so, he wants to destroy the First Amendment? Here is another question for you, Mr. "Fair and Balance," Do you find it OK to send our troops into undeclared wars (strictly speaking is a violation of our Constitution), and getting them killed without defining winning? Is it OK to allow these useless and winless wars to continue forever? For what? Tell me, is it not "OK" to redress grievances against the government, as provided by the First Amendment," and speak out against the killing of millions of unborn babies? And lastly, homosexuality is an abomination, just in case you have not read this in the Bible. Since you profess to be Catholic, I assume you are a Christian and believe the Bible, and understands what the Bible states about sexual perversion.

Again, let me remind you, the reader, to beware of "Phony Conservatives." A phony will talk about how our nation needs to get back to "Constitutional principles," while voting for legislations that is Marxist. They will stand in front of an audience and tell you how great we are; how we should not back down to terrorist and we will win the war against terrorism; they do this without ever defining victory, or defining the terrorist. These hypocrites will talk about principles of our founding fathers, and why we need to return the power to the people; and that they are part of a "grass roots movement," to hold the politicians in Washington responsible; however, what you do not hear them say is, "I am in favor of term limits for all elected officials, and term limits for Federal Judges (if it can be done without adversely affecting the Constitution), with no government retirement plans paid for by tax dollars; and every elected officials income should be reduced 20% per year until government spending is cut;" these phonies are not conservative. If they do not stand for eliminating the pro-Marxist income tax, and getting rid of the Federal Reserve, then they are not Constitutionalist. You will know a person is a conservative when he admits that Republicans like Newt Gingrich, Karl Rove, and George Bush (both of them, Sr and Jr), Dick Cheney, and Fred Thompson are hypocrites and are phony conservatives. If they tell you that they are a Reagan conservative, you will know that they are a fake, a charlatan, and detrimental to true conservatism. If they think that the U.N, has a useful place in the world, and we should continue our support for this corrupt organization, then you will know that they are phonies.

A conservative understands that the government is the enemy of the people. He will oppose the graduated income tax, and the Federal Reserve that has created a currency with no store of value (fiat). A true conservative will not subordinate our judicial system to an international court. A true conservative will not use our military to occupy other countries and will bring our troops home to protect our own borders. If you really want our government to return to the Constitution, read it, understand it, and follow the advice and teaching of Larry Becraft, an attorney who strongly advocates the Constitution and exposes the corrupted powers of government. Stop wasting your vote on incumbents who have served more than six years in office, and do nothing but promote self serving interest. Do not vote for a President to serve a second term. Get rid of local politicians who increase spending; and do not vote for any congressman that adds "pork" to a bill.

PLEASE NOTE: When writing about the IRS, I am not adversely criticizing or demonizing individual employees of the agency. For the most part, the people with the IRS, whom I have met, have been helpful, with a few exceptions. I am sure that most are just family members, just as many of us, trying to do a job. It is the principle of the TAX SYSTEM and the application of the code that I feel is unconstitutional, pro-Marxist, and oppressive.

A true conservative understands that voting is not a right, but a privilege, and that rights are derived from God, whereas, privileges are derived from government. True conservatives will not ask what the government can do for them, but what they can do for government. They detest professional politicians and bureaucrats. Just have a look at Washington, and tell me do these professional insiders ever go away? When you turn on your TV, you will see the same old faces that have been entrenched in the establishment for years. We can't get rid of them. You will see them in some other government job, or they get a job as a "talking head" in the media. Regardless of who is in the White House, the insiders will always have their man there to handle situations and keep the president "under surveillance." The most notorious was David Richmond Gergen; born May 9, 1942, Gergen was an American "political consultant" (whatever that means) and presidential advisor during the administrations of Nixon, Ford, Reagan, and Clinton. He is currently (at the time of this writing) Director of the Center for Public Leadership and a professor of public service at the Harvard's Kennedy School. Gergen is the Editor-at-large for U.S. News and

World Report and the Senior Political Analyst for CNN. It did not matter which party's presidential candidate was elected, Republican or Democrat, Gergen remained at his "post." Leon Edward Panetta (born June 28, 1938) is another one that will not go away. He is the current Director of the Central Intelligence Agency. An American Democratic politician, lawyer, and professor, Panetta served as President Bill Clinton's White House Chief of Staff from 1994 to 1997 and was a member of the United States House of Representatives from 1977 to 1993. He is the founder and director of the Panetta Institute, served as Distinguished Scholar to Chancellor Charles B. Reed of the California State University System and professor of public policy at Santa Clara University. In January 2009, President Barack Obama nominated Panetta for the post of CIA Director; he was confirmed by the full Senate on February 12, 2009 and assumed the office the next day. The list of parasites that are members of the elitist establishment goes on and on: "Oliver North, Dick Cheney, Madeleine Korbel Albright, Howard H. Baker, Jr, Henry Kissinger, Zbigniew Brzezinski, Gen. James L. Jones, Paul A. Volcker, and on, and on, and on!"

I hope the "Tea-Party" survives and is not shanghaied by the Republican Neo Cons. I pray that the people will take back the government, and throw all the rascals out, but I am skeptical, as I already see, the "phony conservatives" trying to get a foothold in the movement. I am concerned when we hold Sarah Palin as the darling of the conservative movement, I am not sure she understands the Constitution and she realizes that our government is operating on principles dictated by Marx and Engels. And, I know Newt is a pseudo Conservative, a Neo Con, corrupt and immoral "politician."

Ending notes and conclusion: **Unfortunately, too many of us are like *sheep*, we simply follow the leader blindly without thinking or searching for the real truth. When someone attempts to tell us the truth and we do not like what we hear, we will dismiss it; or if we hear views contrary to what we want to believe, we will just ignore them. We are willing to "take a person at his word," if we like what we hear. Too many of us will give people running for office the benefit of a doubt and believe candidates when they tell us that they are working for a change in government that will serve our best interest, and that they really want to represent and serve the people; without ever really knowing much about these politicians. Most of us have a need to feel that we can elect candidates who are honest; however, some of us have** discovered that it is best to be skeptical of anything and everything we are told or read even when it comes from so called honest people, or, especially, the media.

In summarizing, I want to go back to the beginning of this book and restate what I said about freedom. All people have a desire for freedom, but freedom has many definitions, and is left up to interpretation, sometimes by those who promise freedom. True freedom begins in the heart and we must distinguish between what it means for us to be free *from* something and to be free *to* do or be something. Man's search for freedom has taken him into the fiercest of protests, struggles, revolutions, civil wars—even world wars. Today, in the midst of free societies, many continue to fight for what they perceive as ever greater freedoms; however, *the great majority of people today are deceived about what freedom truly is!* And yet, we can't be free until we know what freedom is. Neither can we avoid slavery unless we know what slavery is. Are you sure you know?

"They promise them freedom, but *they themselves are slaves of corruption;* for whatever overcomes a man, to that he is enslaved" (2 Peter 2:19; Revised Standard Version). If you are overcome by something, you are *enslaved* to it. What does that mean, exactly? It means that whatever, or whomever controls your life is the element that enslaves you.

Freedom is being physically, financially, spiritually, emotionally, and politically, unobstructed and able to move at will without consequence. As long as you do not interfere with the rights of others, we have a God given right to life, liberty, and the pursuit of happiness, without the threat of government infringing on these rights. Government should be the servant of the people, not their master. Unfortunately, whether we realize it or not, we have allowed government and forces of evils to usurp our freedoms and restrict our rights to move freely, and act freely, even though it does not adversely affect everyone, these elements of power will eventually engulf us all.

When I was child, a teacher told me a story that defines what freedom is. I will tell you this story: "A foreigner arrived to the United States, and gleefully announced his arrival to the land of the free by taking a stroll down the street in his new homeland. As he walked he twirled his cane, and just happened to hit a "yank" in the nose with his twirling cane. The "yank" punched the guy in the face, knocking down the newcomer. The foreigner, staggering to his feet and startled, asked the yank, "Why did you punch me?" The yank replied, "You hit me in the nose with your cane." The foreigner respond with, "Well, this is a free country, I can twirl my cane where and when ever I choose." The yank responded, "Your freedom ends, where my nose begins."

Are we slaves? Slavery did not survive the Civil War, but the ideology of black inferiority that justified slavery in the eyes of slaveholders (and many who were not) certainly did. I have concluded that nothing justifies slavery, even if blacks were inferior, or unable to do anything to free themselves from the chains of slave owners. Like the slave owned by whites prior to the emancipation, blacks are not much better off in a system where they have become economic slaves, just as has most of the middle class, but, especially, for the poor. Today, we have an Elite group of financial tyrants, who control most of the world's resources, including governments. This group sees the majority of the population inferior, and justifies its actions based on their self-proclaimed "god-like abilities" to gain control of global currencies, control the purchasing power of currencies and dictating to the governments what they perceive is in the best interest of the people. This group sees themselves as "gods," and a merciful master to handle problems of the world, including population control and redistribution of property, goods, and services to bring parity to the masses. The prime objective of course, is to establish a system that will serve their needs – "the Power Elite."

Blacks are exploited and used by "elite members" of their own race, considered "leaders," of African Americans. These "black Elitist" will use race as bait in every discussion involving the lack of progress in race relations by re-living slavery. Sharption, Jackson, Farrighan, Wright, and others will do, or say whatever it takes to stir the pot of hatred to keep blacks deprived or least promoting the idea of depravation to remain in a position of power. They use race as a tool to deceive "brothers and sister" into thinking whites are their enemy and it pays off big time. These "exploiters" live a lavish life-style, These so called black leaders also play into the hands of corrupted politician controlled by the Power Elite. By stirring the racial pot, naïve whites and poor blacks, allows legislation to be passed that is detrimental to both races, as it destroys freedoms; such as did the Civil Rights Acts. As I stated earlier in this book, difference should be recognized, and efforts to reconcile these differences should be the main focus rather than forcing views unrealistic, such as "we are the same, the color of our skin is the only difference." This kind of thinking is what enables Jackson, Sharpton, David Duke, and others to prey upon the ignorance of people of all colors and exploit them for personal gains. There are differences, other than color that separates races, and we must understand how these differences affect attitudes, thinking, the ability to govern. We the People must do what we can to improve relationships between people of all races.

Medical Research News provides a complete study on these differences. See:

"The paper, "Thirty Years of Research on Race Differences in Cognitive Ability," by J. Philippe Rushton of the University of Western Ontario and Arthur R. Jensen of the University of California at Berkeley, appeared with a positive commentary by Linda Gottfredson of the University of Delaware, three critical ones (by Robert Sternberg of Yale University, Richard Nisbett of the University of Michigan, and Lisa Suzuki & Joshua Aronson of New York University), and the authors' reply are as follows (for the complete report, go on line and type in name of research paper.

"Neither the existence nor the size of race differences in IQ are a matter of dispute, only their cause," write the authors. The Black-White difference has been found consistently from the time of the massive World War I Army testing of 90 years ago to a massive study of over 6 million corporate, military, and higher-education test-takers in 2001.

"Race differences show up by 3 years of age, even after matching on maternal education and other variables," said Rushton. "Therefore they cannot be due to poor education since this has not yet begun to exert an effect. That's why Jensen and I looked at the genetic hypothesis in detail. We examined 10 categories of evidence."

1. The Worldwide Pattern of IQ Scores. East Asians average higher on IQ tests than Whites, both in the U. S. and in Asia, even though IQ tests were developed for use in the Euro-American culture. Around the world, the average IQ for East Asians centers around 106; for Whites, about 100; and for Blacks about 85 in the U.S. and 70 in sub-Saharan Africa.

2. Race Differences are Most Pronounced on Tests that Best Measure the General Intelligence Factor (g). Black-White differences, for example, are larger on the Backward Digit Span test than on the less g loaded Forward Digit Span test.

3. The Gene-Environment Architecture of IQ is the same in all Races, and Race Differences are Most Pronounced on More Heritable Abilities. Studies of Black, White, and East Asian twins, for example, show the heritability of IQ is 50% or higher in all races.

4. Brain Size Differences. Studies using magnetic resonance imaging (MRI) find a correlation of brain size with IQ of about 0.40. Larger brains contain more neurons and synapses and process information faster. Race differences in brain size are present at birth. By adulthood, East Asians average 1 cubic inch more cranial capacity than Whites who average 5 cubic inches more than Blacks.

5. Trans-Racial Adoption Studies. Race differences in IQ remain following adoption by White middle class parents. East Asians grow to average higher IQs than Whites while Blacks score lower. The Minnesota Trans-Racial Adoption Study followed children to age 17 and found race differences were even greater than at age 7: White children, 106; Mixed-Race children, 99; and Black children, 89.

6. Racial Admixture Studies. Black children with lighter skin, for example, average higher IQ scores. In South Africa, the IQ of the

mixed-race "Colored" population averages 85, intermediate to the African 70 and White 100.

7. IQ Scores of Blacks and Whites Regress toward the Averages of Their Race. Parents pass on only some exceptional genes to offspring so parents with very high IQs tend to have more average children. Black and White children with parents of IQ 115 move to different averages--Blacks toward 85 and Whites to 100.

8. Race Differences in Other "Life-History" Traits. East Asians and Blacks consistently fall at two ends of a continuum with Whites intermediate on 60 measures of maturation, personality, reproduction, and social organization. For example, Black children sit, crawl, walk, and put on their clothes earlier than Whites or East Asians.

9. Race Differences and the Out-of-Africa theory of Human Origins. East Asian-White-Black differences fit the theory that modern humans arose in Africa about 100,000 years ago and expanded northward. During prolonged winters there was evolutionary selection for higher IQ created by problems of raising children, gathering and storing food, gaining shelter, and making clothes. (for Evolutionist)

10. Do Culture-Only Theories Explain the Data? Culture-only theories do not explain the highly consistent pattern of race differences in IQ, especially the East Asian data. No interventions such as ending segregation, introducing school busing, or "Head Start" programs have reduced the gaps as culture-only theory would predict.

Ruston and Jensen also address some of the policy issues that stem from their conclusions. Their main recommendation is that people be treated as individuals, not as members of groups. This is reasonable, until a community is occupied by a majority of a race where IQ's are innately low; in which case, deterioration sets in an entire countries are destitute; famine, disease, starvation, and pestilence becomes a major factor in their everyday lives. Such is the case in Haiti, Zimbabwe, and most of Africa.

Rushton and Jensen are well-known for research on racial differences in intelligence. Jensen hypothesized a genetic basis for Black-White IQ differences in his 1969 Harvard Educational Review article. His later books Bias in Mental Tests (1980) and The g Factor (1998), as well as Rushton's (1995) Race, Evolution, and Behavior, show that tests are not biased against English speaking minorities and that Black-White-East Asian differences in brain size and IQ belong in an evolutionary framework."

I am not an evolutionist. I believe God created the universe and every soul in it. I cannot explain why there are genetic differences in people, or why God created different races, but I accept the fact that this exists, and it is up to us to reconcile our differences, if we are to have peace. We must come together and concentrate on what we have in common and not our differences and we must discredit and disregard those who use hate, suspicion, distrust, and divisional issues to keep us from uniting. For us to survive as "the human race," free from tyranny, and serfdom, we must find a humane plan to control the world's population without genocide, such as abortion, euthanasia, and war. And, we must not be misled by propaganda that serves the Elitist, whose goal is to dominate the world and control its resources, by exploiting racial differences by divisive means.

I have "slammed" Glenn Beck rather hard, and do not want to be unfair. Glenn may be very sincere and really believe in every word he teaches; however, with his resources to investigate and research information, I find it rather hard for him to purport to tell the truth, when the fact are contrary to what he speaks, as in the case of Martin Luther King, Jr. Maybe, Beck feels the real truth would cause blacks to turn a deaf ear to his views, and would get angry with him by exposing the blacks greatest icon as a Marxist and whore-monger; maybe, he feels it is better to use an icon the blacks believe helped them make social and culture gains, in order to get them to take his side on issues, and this is the reason Beck disregards the real truth.. Beck is 100% correct in stating that we must restore our "Christian rights."

I had rather see American come together because we have a common belief in God, and we want freedom, and not because of being misguided by a "phony icon," or because of Beck misguided philosophy. Let's come together because, as individuals we want freedom; the right to really own property, to keep our earnings, and not have the government threatening to take our assets because of unfair and immoral tax laws, which are unconstitutional.

"There's **no art** to find the **mind**'s **construction** in the face." ... from Shakespeare's, "Macbeth."

I cannot look at Beck's face and tell what is in his mind (heart). I do not know him, but I do watch and listen to his "show." I do know that his boss, Rupert Murdoch is said to be a member of the Bilderberg Group and a member of the Council on Foreign Relations, and I am not sure how much of "that influence" Murdoch has in dictating what Beck can say or not say on his show. I do know that Beck and most all of the "talking heads," go to great lengths to discredit anyone attempting to expose "the evil globalist," laughing at them, making condescending remarks about them, and pretending to humor these "poor conspiracy lunatics," when the subject about the New World Order" is mentioned...... oh well, there are about 20 million of the "conspiracy nuts," who really know the truth.

As indicate in my story about the "Yank," and the "foreigner" as long as our freedoms are not interfering on the freedom of others, we should have a right to live a life unencumbered; however, if we allowed others, by consent, or by force, to take control of our lives, we become "slaves." This is happening at a rapid pace. We are no longer free to keep what we earn, as the government has imposed an immoral income tax on our wages; we are no long able to own property, as the government, places a tax on our property and if not paid, the state has the right to confiscate the property; we no longer have the right to pray in public, or express Christian beliefs in the class room for fear of the ACLU; we have no right to protect our borders, as illegal immigration is being ignored; or to barter with gold or silver certificates, as the Treasury Department has made it illegal, and has created a fiat currency..... We have diminishing freedoms with no site in end. How much of our freedoms are we willing to lose before we do something about it? We still have freedoms of thought which cannot be taken away, except by death. Will you die for the sake of freedom?

What is true freedom and how can we have it? In addition to what has already been defined as "what freedom is," I do not want to ignore our freedom as defined by the Bible.

In __Philippians 4:11__ through 13, Paul tells us, "Not that I speak in regard to need, for I have learned in whatever state I am, to be content: I know how to be abased, and I know how to abound. Everywhere and in all things I have learned both to be full and to be hungry, both to abound and to suffer need. I can do all things through Christ who strengthens me."

Many religious people, bureaucrats, politicians, and others like to talk about freedom. But where are they getting their definition of freedom? "And ye shall know the truth, and *the truth shall make you free*" (John 8:32). If they have a different idea of freedom than what is defined by Christ, they are *enslaved*. They are not following true Christianity! And that is true of many who consider themselves very religious.

Jesus said to the religious people of His day, "Well hath Esaias prophesied of you hypocrites, as it is written, This people *honored me with their lips, but their heart is far from me*" (Mark 7:6). Christ condemns a lot of people with this statement! Many people talk about God and Jesus Christ; they act religious, but in truth, their hearts are far from God! They are actually *enslaved* to a false religion and think they are obeying God.

We must be *free* from that kind of false Christianity! And we must be free from the tyranny of Government!!

"For even hereunto were ye called: because Christ also suffered for us, leaving us an example, that ye should follow his steps" (1 Peter 2:21). If you're going to be a Christian, you must follow Christ. If you want to be free from tyranny, follow Patrick Henry's example.

Christ lived His life in perfect subjection to the law of God. He resisted the pulls of His flesh rather than *being overcome* by them! We must remember that God is in control, and put aside our fears and live as "free men."

We need to be like Christ—*free* of human nature! Most people don't even know what human nature is.

"The heart is deceitful above all things, and desperately wicked: who can know it?" (Jeremiah 17:9). That is God's view of human nature, though most people don't believe that. Do you recognize the evil in your own heart—or are you, like most others, *deceived* about human nature? Evil cannot be better illustrated than seen in government's usurping the power of the people through deceit, by making the people think that rights come from government.

We can see this truth illustrated all around us: If you let a desperately wicked heart run free, it will do great damage! We are witnessing a "damaged world" today, caused by evil schemers with one goal, "to control the world."

Memo: "Today Americans would be outraged if UN troops entered Los Angeles to restore order; tomorrow, they will be grateful. This is especially true if they were told there was an outside threat from beyond, whether real or promulgated, that threatened our very existence. It is then that all people of the world will plead with world leaders to deliver them from this evil. The one thing every man fears is the unknown. When presented with this scenario, individual rights will be willingly relinquished for the guarantee of their well-being granted to them by their world government." - Henry A. Kissinger at the May 21, 1992 meeting of the Bilderberg Group in Evian, France. I found this quote on page 84 in Daniel Estulin's book entitled *The True Story of the Bilderberg Group.*

The more I think about this Kissinger quote the more I realize the extent to which we are being lead to the New World Order of "political and financial enslavement" by both the Republican and Democrat Parties. Kissinger made these remarks in 1992. Not much of a stretch to deduce that plans for Middle Eastern chaos were clearly being made as early as 1992 by the international financial elite that Henry Kissinger has pandered to his entire adult life. So how does it play out?

Well, all through the nineties under the Democrat Clinton Administration the stage, entered from the left is being set to draw the U.S. into Islamic conflict. The pot is stirred mightily with the '93 World Trade Center bombing and many other attacks ending with the U.S.S.

Cole. Nothing is resolved, but the stage is set and Kissinger's fearful thoughts are firmly planted not just in U.S. minds, but throughout Europe and the world.

Don't forget that just prior to Democrat Clinton's arrival onstage, New World Order Governance Republican promoter George H. W. Bush allowed Saddam Hussein to go free when our U.S. military was only about 10.5 meters from Saddam's front door (of course, we should not have been there in the first place- Saddam was an ally). Why? Remember how the Treaty of Versailles helped set the stage for World War II? These things are related because they are brought about by the very same entities for the very same purposes. Bush I decorated the stage for the Clinton play to come. The Middle East was put on notice and readied for the pot stirring to begin. Was there any doubt after the Cole attack against our U.S. Navy that things were heating up nicely, just like Henry and his banker buddies wanted?

Enter the George W. Bush Administration, stage right. Nine months into office and WHAM, 9/11. The Towers are down and more people are murdered than at Pearl Harbor. For eight solid years the clarion call of freedom, democracy and self defense shrills in time to the steady drum beat of growing U.S. military force and aggression in the obdurate face of our growing and ever more threatening unseen enemy. An enemy that is at once "nowhere" and "everywhere", even in your own back yard. "You are with us or against us". The flags are waving, the bogeyman is under the bed and the people are angry. How dare these "Muslim rag heads!" Now the seeds planted during the Democrat Clinton Administration, having taken root are being watered, grown and carefully nurtured by the Republican Bush Administration. The Middle East isn't on notice anymore. The Middle East is in utter chaos – just as reliable old Henry postulated. Money is being made hand over fist by Henry's ruthless friends, the American middle class is being bled dry and thousands on both sides are dying. A flotilla of dollars is floating on a sea of blood paddled by our ignorance and we wonder why some folks around the world are unhappy with us.

Enter the unknown, Democrat Barack Obama, stage left, gliding on a media created $750 million dollar swell of "hope and change you can believe in". The counter culture has finally arrived and everything is gonna' be alright. One year later and where are we? Yikes, hope and change took an unexpected, abrupt left turn to Pakistan, Yemen and Iran. (It is a left turn if you're traveling south.) Once again we high-tail it out of Iraq, and why not, it worked the first time – we'll be back. The Messianic Barack and his adoring Tavistockian indoctrinated media are bending over seventeen ways from Sunday to "engage" Iran, the Twelvers and their psychotic followers, or at least to have us think so. They're doing everything possible to head off disaster, but "gosh oh by-golly (terms used by the up and coming star, Sarah Palin)" its real tough going folks. The pot's boiling now. Those elitists are stirring like mad and we're all swirling in a confusing mist of national bankruptcy, personal financial trauma, confusion, fear, patriotism and moral dilemma – just like reliable old Henry told us in 1992… and the money is just rolling in. Does any of this appear accidental to you? Henry's good at his job isn't he?

Most of us missed that last sign post, we were driving pretty fast and probably playing gin in the back seat, but I was watching pretty closely and I'm relatively certain the arrow is pointing straight to Iran and even more chaos and much higher oil prices. Mr. Obama will twist and turn all he can and do his best, but in the end there's going to be a big one and we're going to demand that Barack take our boys and girls to Iran and set it straight. Those doggone rag heads – they're not gonna get the best of us. Oh by the way; did you know that the Federal Reserve Banks collect interest on all this war debt? ("The more wars and the bigger the wars the more debt and the more interest to be collected") Did you know it's their friends and buddies who make the steel and build all the tanks and bombs and uniforms and such? I mean to tell you, "ka-ching, ka-ching" baby all the way to the Bank of London. Ask yourself this question? If you didn't have a greedy central bank to finance all sides of these endless wars up front and then send you the bill after the fact; would you volunteer your hard earned money and your sons and daughters to pay for them? How much would you be willing to spend to kill some guy's family in a far off desert you don't and won't ever meet or know? I didn't think so. We should think about that. Did you ever vote for your kids to be killed or to have someone else's kid killed so some international elitist can get a new yacht? I can't remember doing that. Maybe you can.

We're being had folks. Do any of us really believe that the United States military, without any question the most powerful, best equipped, most highly trained, most heavily armed military in world history, cannot in eight years defeat a bunch of Islamic suburbanites in sandals armed with rocks, rifles and homemade IED's. You're going to have a steep, uphill battle convincing me that we are really trying. Give me a break. A man in a cave is "kickin our ass." "Right." We can explode an armed tank over a distance of miles; a tank we can't even see with the naked eye; but we can't possibly stop a bunch of guys in sandals who train on grade school monkey bars and turn somersaults in the sand. This is a setup and I for one am getting tired of it. Our children are loyally serving in an armed force with the best of intentions, and are being misused as the world police enforcement arm of a bunch of private bankers.

I'm fed up with sending our sons, daughters, fathers and mothers off to war solely to put money in the bank accounts of the "Rockefellers, Rothschilds, Schiffs, Warburgs, Morgans and others on the advice of a flea bitten con man the likes of Henry Kissinger. The bloody sacrifice of our precious families and friends on the altar of Globalist greed and inhumanity for the sake of a group of ruthless, inhuman predators and scavengers has raged out of control and it's time to stop it. NOW is the time to stop it.

How do we stop it? We stop it by supporting and voting for grass roots political candidates who will have the courage and moral turpitude to represent "we the people"; not the international financial interests that presently own the RNC, DNC and all of Washington D.C. We support our grassroots candidates with quarters, dimes and nickels. The global corporations and their putrescent lobbyists can stick their money where the sun doesn't shine. Our candidates will be beholden to no one outside "we the people." These candidates will have to be courageous because the Globalists won't like them, just as they don't like me and they certainly won't like you. Ask Dick Nixon or JFK how things work out when you tell these Globalists something they don't want to hear. We need only to support candidates who have the "guts" to rudely show lobbyists the parking lot.

It looks like a bumpy road ahead, but we have folks on our side who can build one heck of a shock absorber. We are the free love, Boomers who got sucked into the Tavistock dribble and started the "oh so counterculture revolution" back in the sixties. We asked the right questions, but came up with the wrong answers handily provided us by the elite. Well, we ain't kids anymore. It's time to turn in your beads and pull on your boots. They want a REVOLUTION? Let's give 'em one! The TEA PARTY'S (hope we can keep the Republican Party from capturing it), on and I for one am comin' with the biggest cup I can carry.

Is it possible to design and implement a global conspiracy while denying that anyone is engaging in conspiracy at all?

Our future freedom, as American citizens, and all the people in the world depends on the answer to this question, and what, if anything, we choose to do about it.

Let's suppose that you are invited to a meeting and agree to attend. Let's suppose further that you were told the meeting was to begin at 2:00. When you arrive you learn that the meeting has been rescheduled for 2:30 and you were not notified. You are asked to wait, with apologies, in the rather chilly conference room where the 2:30 meeting is to be held. The temperature in the room is for some reason 42°F. After freezing for twenty minutes, the receptionist asks if you would like a sweater. What will your response be? It will most likely be, "yes."

Now let's suppose that the room temperature was 102°F and at 2:20 the same question were asked. What would your response likely be? It will be no thank you. In either case is it at all difficult to predict your probable response? Of course not; the context pretty much pre-determines the outcome.

If you'll bear with me let's do another one. On September 11, 2001, 19 Islamic terrorists died while murdering 2,966 innocent people. When our U.S. Federal government proposed that we ask Americans defend ourselves, what was our pre-determined response likely to be? Defend ourselves of course. Democrats, Republicans, Independents; it didn't matter for most of us. With the possible exception of some Libertarians, we as a people knew exactly what we wanted. Off to Afghanistan we went to set things right. My question for you is: "was this your automatic best response? Or were you led to a particular response and contextually convinced that it was your own?"

I realize it sounds like a stupid question to ask, but since we're in the mood allow me to ask yet another one. Ostensibly U.S. forces attacked Afghanistan to take out Al-Qaeda terrorist monkey bar exercise facilities; I mean training camps hosted by Taliban members. Given that this was fully accomplished within nine months; why are U.S. armed forces still in Afghanistan more than eight years later? What is of strategic interest to the U.S. in Afghanistan? There is no oil. Afghanistan isn't even part of the Middle East. What could possibly be of strategic interest to anybody outside of Afghanistan other than its own intrinsic tribes?

Is it routing and SEC munity for future petroleum pipelines to optimize shipping efficiency? Is it poppy fields and the opium trade? Could it be both? Obviously I don't know; I wasn't invited to the meetings. If Alabama's Infra-guard has a "constitutional supporter's watch list" I'm probably on it, which limits my invitations. Anyway think about this coincidence. The Taliban in conjunction with the Afghan government had successfully reduced poppy production by 94% in 2000 – 2001. Now let's recall that some international central banking families such as the Rothschilds cut their teeth on the opium trade. Of course they don't brag on it so much anymore, but just for such – what's it worth today even though I'm sure no respectable banking family would still be involved?

Well, amid much ado about our U.S. military declaring war on Afghan poppy production upon our arrival in Afghanistan, overall cultivation grew from a record low of 7,606 hectares in 2001 (you know, before we arrived) to 104,000 hectares in 2005 and finally to a new record high of 165,000 in 2006 – no telling how much today's production is {I hope we're spending billions of our stolen U.S. tax dollars on this program because it's really going well. Maybe these same folks could run our new government health care pogrom. Actually they are aren't they?}. Also, note that per UN and IMF records as reported by Global Research, the crop yield per bulb has increased significantly since 2001. No doubt this increase in yield was due entirely too accidental improvements in centuries old growing techniques and not to technical innovation and fertilizers contributed by Western countries. I'm sure that's the case. Also, please note that 92% of all global heroin production originates in Afghanistan.

This little family farm business is worth around $2.7 billion annually to the ripped off Afghan poppy farmers; ripped off, yes, but still not bad for the hill country. How's the city folk do'in? Well let's take a look.

Annual street value for 2006 was estimated to be more than $120 billion U.S. (maybe, twice that today). According to Global Research and Asian Banker, 15 August 2003, IMF estimates global money laundering to be between $590 billion and $1.5 trillion annually – a significant portion of which is garnered from the narcotics trade. The actual numbers are difficult to estimate as bespoke establishments such as JP Morgan Chase, Citibank and Bank of England don't include "such nonsense" in their annual reports. Their hands are washed so no tax is paid either to help offset those highly desirable socialist control programs they're so proud of promoting for us unwashed folk.

If you choose to believe that our sons, daughters, fathers and mothers are dying in Afghanistan due to our "self defense war of necessity" –hey – that's your right. I won't burst your bubble. For my part, I suspect that the political context has been highly and expertly orchestrated so as to lull our inexpert ears into a suspension of disbelief by the manipulative media symphony. Good piece of work too. The Tavistock Institute is worth every central banking penny invested. Now I can't wait until we get to Iran. That's going to be an even bigger, faster downhill carnival ride.

My question is: What other obvious contextual manipulations can you think of that may have effected your impressions and thinking with regard to public policy? Just a few hints to get you started; establishment of the Progressive Federal income tax in 1913; creation of Federal Reserve System in 1913; U.S. entered World War I on April 6, 1917; U.S. and European central bankers funded Bolshevik Revolution in Russia, 1918; 1920 farming/banking depression; 1929 stock market collapse; 1930's depression: U.S. entered World War II on December 8, 1941; Vietnam police action from 1961 to 1975; and a lot more police action in coming years; 2000-2001 tech stock bubble burst; 2008 financial collapse; Now what about the future? The future is "THE NEW WORLD ORDER?" Gerald Celente predicts that we will be a "third world country" by 2012, and he has been right so far in his past predictions.

The (my) Solution:

I would be negligent, if I did not provide a solution to our problems. There is a way to avoid a collapse of our economy, a loss of freedom, and not allow our once great nation from becoming just another third world country, or like Argentina or worse.

<u>Well, we could start with the following:</u>

>*A total elimination of the property tax and the income tax*

>*Dismantling the Federal System – get rid of it (eliminate fiat currency)*

>*Bring our troops home and protect our borders (deport all Muslims, and illegal - and others who do not support Constitutional law - Muslims cannot because of religious beliefs). Kill anyone attempting to enter country illegally.*

> *Cut the number of government employees by 70% and reduce all income of all government employees and retirement funds by 50% (at least), eliminate salaries and retirement funds for all elected officials, and for sure reduce income by at least 50% with no retirement fund for elected officials or judges.*

>*Develop the most destructive weapons possible and use them, if anyone attempts to attack us or even threatens us.*

>*Separate Palestine and give them their own nation. Israel is not to interfere, but once Palestine is completely free, if they attack Israel once - nuke them!*

>*Eliminate public education (let private and church schools educate children and require Constitution to be taught).*

>*Death penalty for: Murder, Pedophiles, Smut peddlers, - no one allowed to use obscene or vulgar language in the entertainment media or in public.*

>*Government's ability to tax should be limited, and any tax should be voted on by the people.*

>*Get rid of most licenses and permit requirements*

>*Let utilities compete for market share.*

>*Every household is required to have a weapon (except for dangerous criminals)*

>*Restore states rights, and even then state's authority should be subordinated to individual rights*

>Get rid of all entitlement programs, and make sure the law is equally applied.

Finally, declare a day of Jubilee, and announce that all individual debt is forgiven. Revalue our currency and establish a store of value for the dollar. Get back to God and the Commandments of Christ.

My most controversial solution concerns the problem with the world's population growth. This is where I agree with the "Elitist." I agree that the world is overpopulated and control of growth is needed. In fact, we need negative growth, but how is this to be accomplished without global euthanasia? I disagree with the methods proposed by the Establishment, which includes, abortion, mercy killing, starvation, disease, wars, etc., etc. My solution is simple. Control of growth should be done before conception occurs, by sterilization. Any woman or man responsible for conceiving a child out of wedlock should be sterilized, if they are on welfare, or in any way supported with tax dollars. In our stupidity, we have allowed the government to reward illegal births. I think that abortion became legal to allow the killing off of unborn babies who were (are) born out of wedlock (mostly blacks), as a mean to control population, but this "backfired," because the government is paying benefits for illegal children through the welfare system; our government has, in fact, encouraged "poverty breeding" to increase. This must stop! The only moral answer I can think of is sterilization, and it should not only be done in the U.S., but done on a "wholesale level" in nations where starvation, disease, pestilence, and over breeding occurs, and in every cases where a woman and man are on welfare, and unable to support a child. The only quick solution I see is a nuclear war, which may be the only answer, as we have waited too late for global sterilization to work, or for sterilization to be accepted as a legitimate, and moral means to control the world's birth rate.

The views expressed herein are my own and should not be considered those of anyone else, unless otherwise stated.

I think I will just end the book here and now!

The End
Final note about myself: I am not a good person, and have committed my share of sin, more so, than most of the people about whom I have written. There is not much "bad" that I have not done, and I am highly critical of

myself. I have done many things that I regret and I am ashamed to admit; however, I do not hold myself up as a righteous person, nor do I capitalize on religion to better my lifestyle. I am admitting that I am not a good person in advance, so, you are pre-warned not to be surprise to learn of my many faults and shortcomings; however, I am a Christian save by the Grace of Jesus, my Lord. I thank Him for dying on the cross that all my sins are forgiven. I do not judge anyone's soul to hell or heaven, as this is God's job. I do, however, judge a tree by its fruits, as Christ has commanded. All through this book, I have honestly attempted to make observations of people of influence ("the good, the bad and the evil"), and expose the truth regarding governments and the economy; if any of my observations, comments, statements, or evaluations on issues, and events are not true, I apologies to the reader, but I do not apologize for expressing my personal views, as it is my First Amendment right, "freedom of speech!"

Please take the time to email me for my research and notes, in fact, you will receive a copy of what was to have been my first book, but because so much of the information was "cut and paste," the publisher would not print it. - Ken Brown (braunkenh@aol.com)

-